YOU DON'T SAY

YOU DON'T SAY

Stories, Poems & a Few Surprises

STEVE THEME

HALYARD PRESS

The following pieces first appeared and are reprinted with permission from their respective publishers: "The Deadliest Year of the Deadliest Catch" *Alaska* magazine, Feb. 2013; "Getting Boiled" *The Timberline Review*, 2015; "Ghost #1: What Did the Old Man Want?" *Weird Reports*, 2018. "Lulu" won the Oregon Writers Colony Nonfiction contest, 2016. "Big Money" won honorable mention in the Kay Snow Fiction Award, 2018.

Author photo by Pierce Thieme, 10/22
Cover and interior design by Vinnie Kinsella, Indigo: Editing, Design, and More.

Published by Halyard Press.

You Don't Say is available in the following formats:

Paperback: 978-0-9863929-3-1
Kindle: 978-0-9863929-4-8
ePub: 978-0-9863929-5-5

To teachers: your teachers, my teachers, all teachers

Life isn't about finding yourself. Life is about creating yourself.

—Bob Dylan

Author's Note

This book consists of pieces written from 1979 to 2022. They were never intended as an anthology, yet here they are. Some pieces have been published nationally, while others are seeing their first light of day.

Although most of the stories here are nonfiction, there are fiction pieces interspersed without any discernible pattern. To eliminate confusion, the author has placed a superscript "F" at the end of the titles of the fiction pieces. If there is no F at the end of the title, then the story is true.

Contents

The Deadliest Year of the Deadliest Catch

The worst disaster in the history of U.S. commercial fishing occurred on Valentine's Day, 1983, when the king crab boats *Americus* and *Altair* sank in the Bering Sea. Fourteen men were lost. I was the last person to see them alive.

I understood calculated risk. In the fall of 1980, I entered my bank in Seattle as a scruffy 22-year-old and plunked down an $11,500 cashier's check (in 2023 that's worth about $40,000), and watched while the pasty middle-aged teller looked down at the check, then up to me, then back down to the check. I'd earned the money in only three months while king crab fishing in the Shelikof Strait off Kodiak Island. So when the phone rang in November of 1982 with a friend telling me one of the crew on his crab boat had just been fired, I took finals early to end a quarter in college and bought a plane ticket to Dutch Harbor, AK.

After two flights and 12 hours in the air I finally saw a thin runway hemmed in by scalloped cliffs on the right, and the sea to the left. A moment before touching down, crosswinds hit causing a hard lurch toward the grey cliffs. The wingtip almost smacked the ground. Dutch Harbor introduced itself.

In a muddy taxi I rattled my way to the Sea Alaska cannery. Walking to the dock I felt the cold mist of all Alaskan ports, and could smell the thick brine of low tide; steam shot the sweet smell of cooking crab from pipes that poked through the cannery's walls of corrugated steel.

Climbing aboard the *Aleutian No. 1*, I came across a man standing on deck. He stood trim to the point of being skinny, and appeared in his early-forties. Because of his age, I realized he was the skipper. To work the deck on a crabber demands youth. "I'm Jostein," he said in a heavy Norwegian accent. "It's good you're here."

"I'm Steve. Good to be here." We shook and I felt the wiry grip of an iron palm.

It was around 4:00 p.m. and the sun laid low. Jostein shouted the command to castoff. Other men emerged from the cabin and we promptly headed to sea. My duffel bag was somewhere, maybe Anchorage, maybe Cold Bay, but it didn't arrive with me. For the next two weeks on the fishing grounds my friend kindly shared his clothes, and I was happy to wear them, even though he was four inches shorter than me.

The boat carried a survival suit for each of us—a red neoprene cocoon that when zipped up squeezed a watertight seal exposing only eyes, nose and mouth. I pulled mine from a locker, folded the arms and legs into a rectangle, walked to the head of my bunk and placed the suit as my pillow. If the boat started going down while I was asleep, I could find it quickly.

We ran 20 hours to reach the fishing grounds, where the top of each wave jettisoned white froth that blew toward a sky the color of headstones. After about eight hours, we had set 100 pots. Running to the next string of pots, already in the water, took less than a half hour. We pulled them and restacked each one on deck. After 16 hours of work we'd caught maybe a dozen crab. I finally got to pee.

Weeks struggled into months and my beard grew to become a gasket against the winter wedging its way between my raingear and neck. With calories burning on deck, and only glimpses of time in our bunks, opportunities to eat remained scarce; each man kept losing weight.

The Alaska Department of Fish and Game recorded more than 160 million pounds of crab caught the year before. By the end of the '83 season the entire fleet brought in only 12 million pounds; biologists learned for the first time that year how quickly crab populations can crash.

Wives were calling for money; boat owners took out loans to buy fuel; crew shares hovered below nothing; dinners of steak shifted to soup, and breakfasts of sausage, pancakes and eggs were replaced with oatmeal—but each man shouldered responsibilities, commitments, dreams, and we kept on. Fishermen fish.

Back pain led one of our men to moan for hours. Between strings of pots we'd strap his feet to the crane hook and hoist him so that he hung upside down, stretching his back. I stood over another crewmember as he fell asleep on deck, wearing full raingear, while crab crawled across his chest. My favorite fantasy became a pot falling on me and breaking my arm, so I could rest. Winter hardened: deeper, darker, colder.

February 13th, 1983, and we had been in Dutch about 60 hours to offload our measly catch. We were tied-up next to the *Americus*, which tied next to her sister ship, the *Altair*. They moored between us and the dock, leaving our crew to walk across those two boats each time we needed to reach shore. With every crossing, we would bump into their crewmembers.

"So how's your season going?" I asked, with the butt of a Camel Filter clamped between my teeth, and my head tucked under a salt encrusted green hoodie.

"We're just getting up here now. It's a pretty late start, but I hear things aren't going so great." He looked even younger than me with a ruddy face and sandy hair styled by the wind.

Smoke blew sideways from my mouth. "That's an understatement."

"My dad's the skipper though," the boy smiled with ruddy enthusiasm, "and he knows how to catch crab."

We needed to load another 20 pots from the dock, but our crane couldn't reach over the two other boat's decks. Our gear arrived around 10:00 p.m., and even though the other guys were plenty busy, about to leave right after us themselves, they agreed to stop their work to help us.

The *Altair* crew picked the pots off the dock with her crane, plunked them on top of the stack of pots on the *Americus*, and her crew swung the pots over and lowered them on our deck. Once finished, the young guy I'd spoken with removed our mooring line from a cleat on the *Americus*.

As he threw me the line he shouted, "We're going to be right behind you. So don't catch our crab!"

"Don't worry," I hollered back. "We're not catching anyone's crab." Each of us gave a short wave, and the freezing dark poured in between our boats.

We traveled through the night, and by mid-morning our crew shuffled around the galley cleaning up after a breakfast. Everything mundane—until Jostein hollered down from the wheelhouse, "Come here! COME HERE!"

The four of us crew ran up the stairs full speed. Once we were in the wheelhouse, Jostein turned up the VHF radio. "All that's showing is the bow sticking just above the water." The voice came from the captain of a freighter on the scene. "Just the tip."

"It's the…" Jostein said. His words rolled slowly from his mouth like heavy stones, "…*Americus*, she's capsized." We all stood, listening, fifty miles from the scene, impotent.

"She's going under," the captain on the radio said with steeled calm. "The bow just went under."

The moment crystallized, frozen within its gravity. Staring at the radio remains burned into my memory; it's black knobs, channel 16 displayed in red numbers, and the tiny green light indicating the power was on. We all stood mute, waiting to hear about the rescue. A lonely breeze whispered through the rigging; weather wasn't angry that day.

Breaking the silence, Yostein said, "They've been hailing the *Altair* for awhile. So far no response."

The radio voice lifted and described life rafts bobbing to the surface. Minutes later, the voice reported with stark efficiency that the rafts were empty.

We were tough guys: king crab fishermen, on the Bering Sea, in the middle of winter, but now we could only manage shallow breathing—our thoughts locked behind stone faces. No tears appeared in the wheelhouse, but we knew once word spread there would be a flood.

During the following week hope remained that the *Altair* remained afloat, but hope disappeared when other fishing boats and aircraft surveyed more than 20,000 square miles in a valiant attempt to find the missing vessel. They found only grey waves.

The National Transportation Board's report is entitled: CAPSIZING OF THE U.S. FISHING VESSEL *AMERICUS* AND DISAPPEARANCE OF THE U.S. FISHING VESSEL *ALTAIR*, BERING SEA NORTH OF DUTCH HARBOR, ALASKA, FEBRUARY 14, 1983. No survivors. Nothing recovered. No one knows why they capsized. I have a theory—it doesn't matter.

Candy bars, coffee and cigarettes powered us through that Valentine's night. But even in the middle of nowhere, we couldn't escape thoughts of the seven, probably fourteen, fishermen who only hours before had selflessly taken time to help us—with my shout between our boats, and them leaving right after us, I suspect I was the last to talk with any of the crew. I thought of what family members would have given to get that last glimpse, that last word.

Two weeks later another boat sank, leaving six more un-marked graves. Another sinking; this time six of the crew were rescued, but the cook, one of the few women in the fleet, didn't make it. Rumors circulated they were one survival suit short. Boats had also gone down in the fall. And as each boat sank that season, I could hear the deep toll of a church bell:

The *Endeavor*...
The *Golden Viking*...
The *Ocean Grace*...
The *Americus*...
The *Altair*...
The others....

Everyone was pushing harder than usual and taking more risks because there were so few crab. By season's end, 44 souls had abandoned their drowned bodies. I estimated about one in eleven crab fishermen had died. This became the year king crab fishing catapulted to the deadliest occupation in the world. Thank God nothing close to this number of seasonal fatalities has occurred since then. Even coal miners in China had a better chance of surviving than us, a way better chance.

Each time we offloaded I called home. On one call I looked at my right hand as I dialed. I'd torn my index finger and blood seeped from under an improvised bandage consisting of a piece of torn T-shirt wrapped with black electrical tape. By then the boat's medical kit contained only dental extraction pliers.

During those calls I never mentioned the multiple times other men, or I, were almost pulled, slipped, knocked or swept overboard. By the end of each call, with my mother on the line,

I made sure she would forever be able to draw some comfort in case these were my last words to her. "I love you."

Since then, the sea has not changed; fishermen have not changed, but after that season the fishery changed, most would say for the better. Seasons are much shorter and crews even wear life vests now. Lives are still lost though and there's no guarantee of money. But as long as there are king crab, and people willing to pay a small fortune to eat them, there will be hard-working men, and a few hardy women, fishing the dark winters, risking it all to realize their aspirations and support their families.

When fishermen leave for the grounds we tell them we love them and wish them good luck. When they return we open our arms. But there are heartbreaking times we get to only honor their memories, and we're forced to catch and release.

Money In

Career Objective: To be obscenely overpaid.

Experience

Shovel Boy, spring 1973. Seattle. The University District YMCA sponsored a bike ride from Seattle to the southern Oregon coast. I saddled up. Gayle Hampton led the trip and afterward she hired me to dig up a part of her lawn to plant a garden. I carved out 150 square feet of hard sod with a dull shovel and made $5.

Day Camp Counselor, summer 1973, University District YMCA, Seattle. Gayle asked if I'd like to work at the Y as a day camp counselor. I'd be responsible for 10 kids to lead around town and try to keep them safe and busy. It paid $45 per week. Being under 16, I needed to get a work permit. (This indicated my parents understood I wasn't being used as child labor, which I was.) At times I was leading groups of kids only a year or two younger than me. Trial-by-fire leadership, which is how all leadership begins.

Day Camp Counselor, summer 1974, U-District Y. At one point in the summer we took about 150 kids on an overnight campout. They ranged in age from first through sixth grades. It rained the entire time, was windy and cold, plus dinner showed up about three hours late: crying kids pushing crying kids, while being watched by kids crying.

Front Desk Clerk, 1974, U-District Y. When the Y asked if I'd like to work the front desk, I jumped at the opportunity to make $2.50/hr. In only two hours I could make five bucks! It may have been minimum wage but felt like rolling in the dough. I ran the front desk on Sunday afternoons, not because I was a management heavyweight, but because I was the only employee in the building. At the time I didn't realize my boss had no idea what she was doing leaving a sixteen-year-old in charge.

Harbor Master, YMCA Camp Orkila, summer 1975, Orcas Island, WA. This camp is in the San Juan Islands and has a ton of shoreline. I ran the dock, gave sailing lessons, taught kids to row and motored out in my rescue boat when kids were having problems. One night while sitting on the bunkhouse porch playing my harmonica, a guy came up and asked if I had another harp and suggested we jam. This man was a friend of another counselor and had made a special trip to camp. He was an NBA player early in his career. They called him Dr. J. (Julius Erving: four-time MVP, won three championships, holds three scoring titles, is the first human to slam dunk a basketball from the foul line—yes, the fucking FOUL LINE!). We jammed as the sun set.

Bag Boy, Lake City Thriftway, fall/winter 1975, Seattle. After school I bagged groceries. On my first day the bald manager asked the balding assistant manager to show me around and get me trained. We walked through the swinging vinyl doors to the storage area in back. The assistant manager picked an egg from a carton, threw it splattering against the brick wall, declared, "I hate this fucking place," and walked away. My training was now complete.

Harbor Master, YMCA Camp Orkila, WA, summer 1976. Camp asked me back. One afternoon a storm kicked-up and I brought the kids off the water. One boy was almost a mile off-shore and his sailing pram wasn't going to make it back so I set off in my rescue boat. In about half a mile my engine ran out of gas, and he was still being blown out on growing seas. I had 100 yards to reach the boy so I broke out the oars. At least we could be together as we were swept into the Strait of Georgia. I pulled with all my might to reach him and on about the third stroke my starboard oar snapped in half. We were both adrift in a gathering storm, with no radios. As it turned out, Frank Herbert, the author of the *Dune* science-fiction series, lived in a beach home next to the camp. He jumped into his skiff, then raced out and saved our lives.

Ad Copywriter, an ad agency, Seattle, spring 1976. A friend of mine worked at an ad agency and the owner mentioned they needed a copywriter for the Chateau Ste. Michelle winery US bicentennial celebration. My friend told them she knew a good writer. A more accurate description would have been she knew someone who likes to write. She may not have mentioned I was a junior in high school. They primarily wanted a slogan. I came up with, Freedom of the Press—tongue in cheek, but it's a winery, not a mortuary. They chose Grown in Freedom's Soil. (blah)

Carpet Cleaner, Cory's Cleaners, Seattle, winter/spring 1977. During the beginning of my senior year in high school classes were only in the afternoon, so I got a job cleaning carpets for the first half of the day. My partner, Robert Roberts, was a man who immigrated illegally from Mexico and learned to speak English while enlisted in the US Marines. The main drawback to this job was going from work to school while still wearing my cleaning uniform. The pants made me look like a bell boy, which generated a number of comments.

Halibut Long-Liner, Fishing Vessel *Jade*, Seward, AK, summer 1977. I had earned enough credits to graduate early my senior year, so three days after the first semester ended I boarded a ferry on the Alaska Marine Highway bound for Hanes, Alaska. Eventually I hitchhiked to Seward and got on a ratty green halibut boat where it was just the skipper and me. We caught a lot more than just halibut and I learned that hours after you cut off a wolf eel's head it can still bite you. I'd have rows of heads hanging before taking them off the hooks.

Jumbo Prawn Fisherman, FV Jade, Seward, AK, summer 1977. After halibut season we fished for spot prawns at the base of a towering glacier. The night of my senior prom I was hunting/poaching seals in Aialik Bay and turning them into shrimp bait. Eventually the skipper lost his mind and stood on the foredeck screaming gibberish—some screaming at the mountains, some directed at me. (His wife later blamed this on his diabetes.) While the veins in his face were still bulging red I saw a seaplane fly through a gap in the distant mountains. The plane headed toward us, landed, and taxied up to the boat. The skipper calmed down but we didn't know what was going on. The pilot came from the cannery and was just checking on our catch. This took us by surprise. I tossed my duffle bag into the cockpit and flew away.

Box Maker, Sea Alaska Products, Seward, summer 1977. Made wooden boxes to hold salted salmon roe destined for Japan. I slid completed pine boxes down a ramp to the roe room, where only women were allowed to work. This roe is by far the most commercially valuable part of a salmon, and it's almost never sold in the US.

Salmon Fisherman, FV *Sativa*, Kodiak, AK, fall 1977. A drunk guy laying in the bushes in Homer, Alaska told me there were a lot of fishing boats in Kodiak. So, I headed out there, and for my first trip onto the docks I saw two guys fighting. One was the skipper and he was kicking a drunk crewman off the boat. The skipper won, so I asked him if he needed a new deckhand. As he left for the bar he turned and shouted, "Oh yeah, you're also the cook." I didn't know how to cook.

Cook, College Inn Pub, Seattle, 1978. It was nice to have a job where I could eat. The patrons were mostly students from the University of Washington, which I was attending. If someone wished to split legal hairs, I shouldn't have been hired for this job, since I was underage. (Hey, they never asked how old I was.)

Night Janitor, Lake Union Building, Seattle. 1978. Wipe, clean, vacuum and empty the used tampon receptacles. A deaf man and I spent the night cleaning this six-story office building. Student during the day, majoring in Technical Writing.

Busker, Key West, Florida, summer 1978. The Sunset Celebration in Mallory Square was a nightly freak show of jugglers, jewelers, jammers, and gypsies. (Today, the ritual is codified by the city and antiseptic.) I played harmonica there and earned enough for food.

Carpenter's Helper, Key West, summer 1978. As I walked by a bar that was being renovated, I poked in my head and asked the carpenter if he needed help. He paid me $10/hr. I was in Key West as part of a 7,000-mile solo hitchhiking odyssey. That trek eventually became the story for my first book.

Fry Cook, Skippers, Seattle. 1978. Fish and chips anyone? This was the first job where I was fired. (Tossed some old shrimp in a garbage can and they wanted to sell it the next day.)

Skittles Pied Piper, Seattle, 1978. Walking through neighborhoods I'd deliver free samples of Skittles packs in clear plastic bags that I hung on doorknobs. When I came across groups of elementary-aged kids they all got Skittles. One group followed me for a while.

Shipyard Laborer, Lake Union Shipyard, Seattle, 1979. Worked the swing shift at this rusty shipyard. Every payday the foreman drove his black Caddy into the yard, with his wife in back, and whored her out for $20 a blow. I was a contract worker and never actually saw her, but the permanent guys were expected to pony up. Student at the UW during the day.

Salmon Tender Crewman, FV *Sea Quail*, Kodiak, AK. 1979. I got on the Sea Quail in Everett, WA and we sailed to Kodiak Island. Over the summer we acted as a salmon tender, taking fish from smaller fishing boats, and when our refrigerated hold was full, we'd haul them to the cannery.

King Crab Fisherman, FV *Sea Quail*, Kodiak, winter, 1979. Dropped crab pots thousands of times in the Shelikof Straits.

The *Sea Quail* was a converted tuna boat and it sat low in the water. At outdoor fishing shows in the Pacific Northwest you can still go to the Coast Guard booth and see a pic of this boat being covered by a wave. On one clear-crisp day I made $1,500 (equal to around $6,000 in 2023.)

Unloader, United Parcel Service, Seattle. 1980, From midnight to 4 a.m. I unloaded UPS long-haul trucks. As a purely physical act this was harder than crab fishing on an hour-by-hour basis. But the days weren't twenty hours long, and nobody got killed doing it. Student during the daylight.

Boat Mechanic/Janitor, Honolulu, HI, 1980. Each morning I cleaned and maintained the equipment on a commercial sailing trimaran that took tourists for night cruises off Waikiki Beach.

Junk Yard Dog, Sand Island, HI. 1980. Worked in a blazing-hot junkyard, stripping cars of their engines and transmissions. Thanh, a young refugee from Vietnam, worked with me and we were paid in cash at the end of each day. We both wore rags but he looked worse because he was so thin. After enduring the war, it took him three years to reach the US via squalid refugee camps in Thailand and Malaysia. Today, I see him as the one standing huge on Liberty Island, holding high the torch of freedom.

Diesel Mechanic, Ke'ehi Boat Harbor, HI. 1980. I was living on a sailboat and got a job at the harbor working as their resident mechanic. The marina was located at the end of the main runways for the Honolulu International Airport. We were so close that everyone had to stop their conversations and stand in awkward silence whenever a plane took off.

Sailboat Delivery Crewman, O'ahu/Maui/Moloka'i, HI. 1980. Delivered multiple sailboats between the islands. One skipper was a young retired guy who'd made his money in Miami as a cocaine cowboy. Under my mattress he hid an M16. The guy was a selfish idiot and a lousy sailor.

Sailboat Delivery Crewman, SV *Sorcery*, Honolulu, HI–Marina Del Ray, CA. 1980. I had no money to get home, so I walked the docks at the Ala Wai Harbor and found a boat sailing to California the next morning. One of their crewmen had broken his arm that afternoon and a spot was open. Crossing the Pacific under sail became holy. I didn't get paid directly, but the crew got a celebration night in Long Beach on the *Queen Mary*.

Sheetrock Sherpa, Seattle. 1981. This involved carrying/running sheetrock, one sheet at a time, into offices and homes under construction. There were almost always stairs and landings involved. Everyone who did this work had bad backs, even though they were young. I got out before it got me.

Cook, Dantes, Seattle. 1981. This bar was loaded with students from the University of Washington. I broke up one fight by letting the pugilists continue to pummel each other while I spread my arms out, pumped my legs like when I played as a football lineman, and drove them both out the front. Just as we exploded out the door, the cops were on the other side reaching for the handle. I kind of delivered the drunks right into their faces. Kept going to school during the day.

Landscaper, (I don't recall the company name.) Seattle. 1982. I was on a crew that installed rock walls at commercial construction sites. Each morning we met at the Rimrock Café on Lake City Way where we got our marching orders. A friend and I commuted to the sites on his Honda 450.

Horse Camp Counselor, Skookum Flats, WA. 1982. The Y called and asked if I could be the counselor for a two-week horse camp by Mt. Rainier. Camp consisted of a dozen kids and three adults. I was responsible for the kids, another young man was responsible for the horses, and we had a real adult to cook and watch over all of us. We slept in tents next to a primitive coral in the forest. If a horse had issues that day, it was assigned to me. My favorite had a trick of running full speed under low limbs to knock me off. I never took a tumble, but since I knew what he was doing, I'd let him blast off at an emergency airstrip to get his ya-ya's out.

Driver, Seafirst Bank. Seattle. 1982. The internet didn't exist and to transfer financial data from one location to another I drove tapes between Seafirst locations on a graveyard shift. Once I got off this job at 8 a.m. I'd ride my bike to my second job at the pub.

Janitor, College Inn Pub. Seattle, 1982. It took about two hours to clean-up the pub from activities the night before. I would also wakeup Liebert Hemmingway III, (no one knew his real name) a forty-something who fancied himself an adventurer and slept in the utility closet. To this day his beer bottle and my pool cue, crossed like an X, are etched into the stucco of a wall we built by the kitchen. Once everything was clean, I'd peddle onto campus and start classes.

King Crab Fisherman, FV *Aleutian No. 1*, Bering Sea. Winter, 1982–83. Hard fishing—dark, rough, and endlessly cold. The entire fleet caught almost nothing and it became clear the crab population had collapsed. This became the deadliest season in the history of king crab fishing on the Bering Sea. At one point I had to borrow $200 to fly home.

King Crab Fisherman, FV *Arctic Rose*, Bering Sea. Spring 1983. Switched boats and crab species, then pots finally started coming up full. (There are four different species that are sold as king and snow crab.) On deck I worked with an older Aleut man, George Petrokoff, raised on the Aleutian chain. I'm fairly certain he is the only American to be held as a POW in WWII *and* Vietnam. As a child he watched his village burn from the deck of a Japanese frigate. He spent his prime years as a young man—six of them—caged in Vietnam.

Warehouseman, Ballard, WA. Marine Construction and Design (MARCO). 1983–84. I picked components that were assembled into equipment for king crab boats.

Motor Coach Commander, Royal Highway Tours, Skagway, AK. Summer 1984. Drove large tour buses with passengers from cruise ships and carried them into the Yukon Territory, offering commentary along the way. Most people are unaware the Yukon is as large as California, has a total population of one small town (30,000) and 25,000 of them live in one small town. While walking along Bennett Lake with a Quebecois beauty she told me of how the largest rainbow trout in the world was caught right where we were looking at each other with goo-goo eyes.

Bartender, College Inn Pub, Seattle, 1984–85. This time when they hired me I had at least reached legal drinking age, which may, or may not have helped my studies.

Day Camp Director, Downtown YMCA. Seattle. Summer 1985. I led a staff of day camp counselors and about 100 inner-city kids. I became the arbiter of many disputes and learned how differently two sides of the same story can be presented. One little girl said with great affection that I reminded her of her father. I saw him once: grimy tank top, gut hanging out, stinking of booze.

Technical Writer, TOM Soft, Tukwila, WA. 1985. My professional career began when I landed a paid college internship at The Office Manager (TOM) Soft. They developed accounting software, and I edited their user manuals, finding it impossible to believe real human beings would ever read anything I edited. During a slow afternoon, I typed a short story and mailed it to a friend. He took a magnet and stuck the page to a refrigerator where he worked in the kitchen of a large hotel in Kaanapali, Maui. He said the whole staff loved it. The story described that when my manhood gets lively the magnitude of its enormity throws a wobble in the earth's orbit. (Picture the earth as a beach ball, yet it has a baseball bat protruding from it.) This became the first piece I wrote that the public ever read.

Technical Writer, Volt Technical Staffing/Boeing Computer Services (BCS), Bellevue, WA. 1985–88. I finally earned my BA in technical writing and worked at BCS as a contractor writing user manuals, functional specs and programmer guides. PCs had yet to be networked. To print something meant walking down the hall carrying the 5 1/4 inch floppy disk, inserting it into the only PC hardwired to a printer, and typing in the DOS command to copy the file to Port LPT1. Courier was the only font. Screens displayed in amber *or* green. We were considered cutting edge.

Tech Writer/Marketing Staff, North American MORPHO Systems. Tacoma, WA. 1988–90. This start-up company produced some of the first fingerprint identification software for law enforcement. We helped catch criminals and that felt good. I got the company on the front cover of the top national law enforcement magazine and it appeared I had a knack for marketing. When hired I was employee 65. In a year we grew to 300-plus. Unfortunately, we'd sold more than we could fulfill, leading management to keep only people in manufacturing. One morning I walked in and there were armed guards by the HR offices. By the end of that day the company was down to fewer than 100.

Communication Specialist, Boeing Commercial Airplane Group (BCAG). 1990–94, Seattle. Boeing hired me and I wrote training materials, department newsletters and regularly contributed feature articles to the *Boeing News*. At one point there were 500 of us in a converted airplane hangar with zero windows. Half of the people sat at desks in a single open bay with no cubicles or dividers. The phone system featured only three ringtones. Every desk had a phone. Whenever one rang about a third of the population twitched.

Public Relations Manager, BCAG, Renton, WA. 1994–97. Led the international public relations and marketing efforts to launch the 737 Next Gen family. Also acted as a company spokesman for 737 accidents worldwide, representing the company for accidents that took a total of 744 lives. While delivering crisis communications I appeared on media outlets including, CNN, NPR, Dateline, the *New York Times, Nikkei Shimbun, South China Morning Post, Handelsblatt, Newsweek*, and even the *Tundra Drums* of Bethel, Alaska. Wrote weekly speeches for Gordon Bethune (soon-to-be CEO of Continental Airlines) worked directly with Alan Mullaly (future CEO of Ford) and Phil Condit (future CEO of Boeing). Boeing is a good company, but for me it felt a bit slow.

Sr. Public Relations Manager, Waggener Edstrom, Bellevue WA. 1998. WagEd was Microsoft's PR agency and I supported the MS Developer Tools group. Participated in national press and analyst tours for the initial product launch of Visual Studio that featured the first Integrated Development Environment (IDE), which permanently changed how software developers approach creating applications. It was becoming clear to me that I was repeating a pattern of getting bored in jobs more quickly than I would hope, and leaving whenever I identified an opportunity to make more money.

Global Product Launch Manager, Compaq Computer Corp. Houston, TX. 1999–2002. Led an international team to develop enterprise product launch strategies. Launched more than 300 products globally. Wrote whitepapers and led promotional tours. Articulated new strategies to analysts and media. There were eight product divisions and they rarely spoke. My job was to make it look like we had an integrated product approach. The Internet Bubble was inflating, everyone was becoming a trillionaire, which sounded like a good idea to me, but for some reason Compaq's stock was stuck in a long-term stagnation, while I felt a pull to return to the Northwest.

Director of Marketing Communications, World Wide Packets, Spokane, WA. 2003. This was the first company to develop telecommunication equipment that allowed voice/video/data to be delivered simultaneously. I led branding, video production, advertising, PR, tech writing and tradeshows. Upon walking in I was employee 60. In a year we were over 300. The Internet Bubble burst, and in one day the company shrunk back to about 60.

Business Development Manager, Thomas, Dean & Hoskins, Civil Engineers. Spokane, 2004. Somehow I got hired to represent this civil engineering firm to prospective clients. Won some business. Never mind I knew nothing about civil engineering.

Sr. Manager, Demand Generation, Americas, Tektronix. Beaverton, OR. 2004–2009. (Applied for 248 positions before landing this. Tough hi-tech economy.) This company developed electronic test and measurement equipment. Led a team responsible for advertising, direct mails, product launches, tradeshows, webcasts, white papers, videos and sales materials. Increased overall North American sales leads while reducing cost per lead by 50%. The company was acquired and one of the first departments that gets chopped for efficiency is usually Marketing. I found another company just before chopping started.

Director of Marketing, Inspiration Software. Beaverton. 2009. This company developed educational software. After being hired,

I learned the president and CEO were once married, had divorced, but still maintained side-by-side offices. Senior staff meetings consisted of forty-five minutes of her berating him, while reserving the remaining fifteen minutes to yell at the rest of us. They went through five marketing directors in five years. This was the second job I was fired from.

Director of Marketing, Dotster, Vancouver, WA. 2010. Responsible for all corporate revenue generated from 15 web properties that sold subscription software products and domain names. Led a multi-discipline marketing team. I had been unemployed prior to this job and things were getting tough. My mother in-law prayed a novena for me; she prayed nine times per day for nine days that I get a job offer. On the last day of her novena, after 10 months of being unemployed, Dotster offered me this job. (Thank you, Ann.) This company was also a gem and churned through five marketing directors in five years.

Family Service Counselor, Skyline Memorial Gardens, Portland, OR. 2011. Morticians—these days they're called Funeral Directors—are kind people, not creepy necrophiliacs. This job was in a funeral home located in a cemetery. Here I sold funereal products and services. It paid minimum wage until commissions kicked in. This was a short stint but it still hit hard at my self-image of being highly skilled. There wasn't much money, but I gained a quiet pride in knowing that to support my family I was willing to work around dead human bodies, in a cemetery.

Director of Publicity, Inkwater Press, Tigard, OR, 2011–12. Drove retail and consumer book sales. Created social media and advertising campaigns. Wrote website copy, blog posts, press releases and pitch letters. Helped authors distill their books into compelling blurbs. This was an enjoyable position; however, it paid less than previous unemployment benefits.

Digital Marketing Manager, AutoBidMaster, Portland, 2012. Contracted to design and execute marketing activities for this e-commerce auction site for salvage cars. Developed messaging that drove a 100% improvement in the ratio of Preferred registrations to Starter registrations. This was a company of about a dozen people. I was the only one who didn't speak Russian.

Sr. Manager, Email Marketing, Regence Blue Cross/Blue Shield. Portland. 2013–17. Wrote and designed the member-facing emails for Washington, Oregon, Idaho, and Montana. This job eventually became nothing but spreadsheets and data, and that's not what I was hired for. This is the only place where I've ever just stood up and walked out. (When fishing on the Jade, technically, I flew out.)

Director of Marketing, AutoBidMaster, Portland. 2017. Shortly after I left Regence, ABM called me out of the blue and asked if I wanted to work there again. Not really, but I didn't have a job.

Sr. Marketing Manager, First Tech Federal Credit Union, Beaverton, OR. 2017–20. Developed and executed all marketing and acquisition strategies for the Investments and Insurance divisions. Ensured all deliverables launched on time and on budget, while meeting performance goals. Unfortunately, or maybe fortunately, I just couldn't do this anymore. My wife of 32 years had passed away recently and corporate work felt meaningless. I didn't want to do anything just for money ever again.

Independence Day, Fourth of July, 2020. First day of retirement. Well, this is new.

Publisher/Some Guy, Halyard Press, Portland, OR. Independence Day–Present. Spend some time writing, some time thinking, some time being of service; to my knowledge there's never been an oversupply of helping hands. And occasionally, I'll just sit on my front porch and watch hummingbirds fight over the jasmine.

Guest Preacher, Cedar Hills United Church of Christ, Portland, OR. 2021–22. I preached three sermons, although I'm not ordained in any religion. Didn't know the church was going to pay me, but since they did this makes the list.

The Honey Bucket Incident

The day started like every Thanksgiving in Portland—gray, wet and cold. Since this is a holiday about reconnecting with loved ones, my wife and I thought it would be a good idea to have my entire family over. To help ensure there was plenty of togetherness, all 16 of us were spending the night at our house.

Family began arriving and as each car unloaded, everyone present came to the driveway for welcomes and to help carry in festive items. The last to arrive were my parents, which seemed fitting since they were the senior arrival and deserved the grand entrance.

My father viewed himself as a hard-driving man, not just figuratively, but literally. When driving, he was there to drive, not to engage in frivolous activities—activities like stopping to pee. He'd stop when mom needed, but to maximize his time behind the wheel he'd taken to peeing into various bottles while zooming around America's highways. This wasn't the result of an older man's less robust bladder; he'd done this when younger as well. You wouldn't ever want to sneak a sip out of his Coke can or iced tea when he pulled up.

My wife and I, my two sisters and their husbands, a bevy of kids and two dogs were already in the driveway when my parents arrived. It became clear, even before opening his door, that my father was agitated. One of his loving grandsons, eight-year-old Jensen, ran up to the driver's side ready to regale him with fanfare as he exited the car. The door swung open and my father's hand jutted out holding a large bouquet of colorful flowers wrapped in a plastic funnel. "What a nice gift," my wife commented. "We'll put them on the dinner table." He shook his fist some and it was clear he wanted Jensen to take them. With a smile only an adoring grandson can effervesce for his pop-pop, Jensen grabbed the flowers and stepped back. No words had come from my father's mouth before handing Jensen this package, no special instructions as to how he might want to hold it, and without such instructions, things began leaking.

It quickly became apparent there had been no spare bottles rolling around on the car floor that afternoon and the only available vessel became the plastic wrapped around the bouquet.

Jensen jumped back, extending his arm out as far as possible, as my father now warned him of the contents. My wife said maybe these won't go on the table. We all stood in shock as one of my sisters, who happened to be Jensen's mother, snatched the smelly bag, at which point the leak became a pour. Jensen wouldn't be wearing his shoes in the house. He might not have worn them ever again.

My mother, a short round woman, stepped from the car and after 40 years of marriage threw her hands in the air, "Can you believe it?" We all said that no, we can't. "It's just a good thing we had the flowers." The flowers found their way to the garbage can and I hosed off Jensen's shoes.

With everyone present, our lovely house—clean and comforting—now had the ambiance of an airport runway. My father, who taught us that when others are talking the best way to be heard is to shout, was leading the chorus of people trying to be heard. The kids were in the formal living room playing something like soccer/baseball. The other adults were nibbling delicate appetizers while shouting, and I was standing next to a barbeque, in the dark rain, roasting a turkey that was bred to be heat-resistant.

Once the turkey relented, we all gathered around the table, joined hands, and said grace. Three generations gathered with only one person speaking. God's power is truly mighty.

I got to sit at the grown-ups' table. The spread was incredible and we were all genuinely thankful to live in a prosperous, free country, and for all the wonderful food on the table—with one exception. My mother was a traditionalist and liked Thanksgiving food to be made from scratch and slow cooked. Well, one of my sister's signature dishes was canned yams with Jiffy-Puffed marshmallow cream poured on top. Mom cupped her hand to my ear and said, "They looked like damn orange traffic cones in a snowstorm." Every now and then I could see her give it the evil eye. We could hear the kids laughing in the other room and our dogs were using their chairs like slalom poles, making sure any dropped food became quickly appreciated.

Once we finished feasting, I waddled over to the living room carpet where I flopped down on the floor and got in touch with my inner beached whale. After a time, it dawned on me that I was still the host, so I rolled on to my back and bellowed, "Who wants to go for a walk?" Looking around, it appeared an entire pod of whales had beached.

Once out the door the kids sprinted ahead and we marine mammals paddled along behind. While walking down the streets I looked in horror at the early Christmas lights. I let others know our lights weren't up yet to save electricity, the planet, plus the human race, and that I'd be accepting my Noble Prize shortly.

After a couple blocks we came to an area with homes under construction. The kids wanted to run through some of them, but it was dark and we decided that wasn't such a good idea. So instead, as a much better idea, seven of them spontaneously rushed into the construction workers' honey bucket and closed the door. Shouts of glee came from inside but the adults felt this might not be the best playground environment either. What happened next has gone down in family lore as, "The Honey Bucket Incident."

My father, stately old gentleman that he was, went running to the back of the honey bucket, raised his arms over his head like a mad chimp and started banging on it. He then proceeded to holler like an angry German imitating Freddy Krueger. The kids, who were jammed into this pitch black, smelly little box, erupted out the door screaming. (It was at this instant the un-disputable genetic link between my father and his grandchildren surfaced, as they too ran with chimp arms waving over their heads hollering oddly-German Freddy Krueger noises.)

Although they were no longer packed in the outhouse, there was one problem. The first one out the door, my sweet little nephew Hunter, had tripped and landed face first in the slop that lives in front of every construction site toilet. His luck took a further turn south when his plight didn't impede the others. In their haste to escape, the rest of the kids managed to trample Hunter. Adding insult to injury, on his cheek, like a kiss from a woman wearing brown lipstick, was a perfect tennis shoe print made of honey bucket floor drippin's. What had started as an effort to get out of the house and avoid turning into human Jell-O was now more like a scene in a disaster movie: crying kids running everywhere and frantic parents.

The adults were scolding, shouting things like, "What were you thinking?" The kids were shouting things like, "Alex stuck his hands down there." We checked Alex's hands and had yet another reason to be thankful…he hadn't found anything, and no one asked what he was searching for.

Once back at the house Hunter got a thorough scrubbing and the rest of us did as well for good measure. We ate dessert, watched some TV, ate dessert again, and went to bed. The night, like all Thanksgiving nights, although this one was special with 16 of us, launched into vigorous try-outs for the US Olympic Snoring Team.

Sailing

Three sheets to the breeze
My mates and I, a few clouds
In an ocean of sky.

Rain

Drops snake down the window
Weaving beaded vertebrae in their wakes
Bones of the sky falling

Lulu

Standing in the middle of the middle of America, I found myself in a town that I thought existed only in old Jimmy Stewart movies. From Main Street I could see white picket fences protecting deep green lawns. Huge oaks lined every lane. A white gazebo with lattice sides sat on a small grassy plot in the center of the town square. Beside the square, Roman columns presided over white marble stairs leading to dark courthouse doors. Next to the courthouse sat City Hall, a simple square building planted firmly, stone walls reflecting a solid people. As a bookend to City Hall rested the church, pure white, offering a spire that rose above all else. I half-expected a silver-haired woman to beckon from a doorway holding a warm plate of chocolate chip cookies, her white apron and floral dress neatly covering a matronly frame.

"Jesus Christ, I hate this," a young woman snapped once I stepped into her black VW Bug. She brushed black stringy hair from her eyes, took a look at me, and said, "I'm Lulu."

* * *

I didn't squander my youth on responsibility. In April of 1978 I struck out on the road, carrying a small backpack filled with clothes, a Buck knife, two harmonicas and a map of the US. I was nineteen and had just finished my first quarter at the University of Washington, where I learned the lecture halls were more anti-septic than I could tolerate. Classmates squealed about parties and cars, and I couldn't stop viewing them as pampered pets. Watching my bad attitude get worse, I needed to do something.

That something unfolded into a 7,000-mile hitchhiking trek. Before the trip ended, I had careened across America, twice, the long way: from Seattle to Key West, Florida, then a month in the Keys, before hitching back to Seattle. Rides came like rogue waves, unexpected, with force, and then vanished.

* * *

"Hate what?" I wasn't sure if she meant the weather, her car or just life.

"All this…Pollyanna." Her arm made a sweeping motion to point out the buildings, as her black fingernails grated across the town. "You know a lot of sick things go on in these pretty white boxes."

Her thick black overcoat sprouted frayed ends from the cuffs and around the collar. I couldn't tell if she wore pancake makeup or if her skin shone that ghostly. Her eyes looked like white planets surrounded by the empty space of mascara. A black leather skirt led down to black nylons showing oyster white legs through the tears. Worn black tennis shoes stomped on the clutch pedal and accelerator.

The backseat encased layers of her life. On the bottom squatted cardboard boxes from a liquor store. Above those were bulging plastic bags, stretched and torn by the sharp corners of their loads. Topping the pile were clothes, still on the hangars, as if they had been bear-hugged out of a closet and tossed there. They projected a musk of wet fabric that filled the car.

She railed against the manicured world as we drove past ornamental gardens, sidewalks, well-dressed people—all received her caustic glare and comments. Eventually her steam started running out, and she began to talk.

"I'm an actress in Manhattan. Been there about two years, but it's tough." Her voice softened and she didn't seem as concerned with society's oppressive hypocrisy. Picket fences kept guiding us down the streets. "I grew up around here," she said under her breath.

"Looks like an okay place," I said, knowing she'd come back with a different opinion.

"Yeah, it's great if you like having to hide everything in your fucking life." She didn't elaborate, but followed by saying she didn't miss her dead father.

I told her when I attended grade school I lived in New Jersey, and that my family would take day trips into Manhattan and go to the museums. "Manhattan is pretty much the definition of a great place to visit, but I wouldn't want to live there." Listening to myself, I sounded like a hick.

"No, it's not really that great." She let out a long exhale and ran a hand over her hair. "I've got a place. It's small but I share it with two guys. They're actors too." Adjusting the rearview mirror she checked her face. "We've got a radiator." She looked down a quiet side street where a little boy and girl rode their bikes. "All kinds of people in the city, every type there. Not like these Wonder Bread towns." Then giving her head a twitch that flipped the black hair from her face, she said, "It kinda surprised me. It's so big ya know." But it seemed clear that's why she left the Midwest, to get culturally and geographically as far away as possible.

"There's lots of competition," she continued. "Some of those girls have been to acting classes." Envy and disdain mixed in her voice. "I've been thinking about it some." Sitting at a red light she looked down at her hands, and then with a blank stare evaluated her clothes. "I can sing too."

I kept quiet, letting her thoughts range. "My parents wanted me to be a straight stick, to look and act like the other kids." She turned to me and let out a short blast of breath while shaking her head. "My mom and dad talked about how nice it would be when I get married. You know, kids, dogs, white fence. The whole schmear." She laughed. "They thought that would make me happy."

Rain began falling and she waited a bit before turning on the wipers. "What made me happy was my mom's cooking. God, that woman could cook."

Lulu didn't strike me as the type who cooked much.

"I can't believe it," she said slowly. "Mom actually would put hot pies next to an open window to cool."

This was the first time I'd seen a hint of a smile. Not a light smirk or quick lip lift, but a slow lasting hint. She turned and gazed at me, as if to say "See, I can smile."

"That's like the old Sunday comics," I said, thinking of the Katzenjammer Kids. She already thought I came from Bumpkinville, so I kept being corny. "The kids always snuck up to the window and would steal the pie."

"Yeah, I tried that once." Her smile broadened a bit, "burnt my fingers." The crow's feet creasing the corners of her eyes smoothed as her face relaxed, revealing her youth. Many of the homes and shops now received long looks from her, fixing her gaze on them as we passed.

She pulled to the side of the road. "This is it. I'm not going any farther." We sat at nondescript cross street. Lulu leaned forward a bit and turned her head to get a better view out of the passenger window. Raising her arm and pointing, she said, "My mom lives down this block."

I nodded, but her statement surprised me. Until now she hadn't mentioned anything about seeing family. Before getting out, I had to ask, "So if this place is so crappy, why are you here?"

She clamped down, quite for a while. "My cousin called a couple days ago. Mom's sick. Really sick." She blinked, but her mascara still smeared down her cheeks. "She needs someone to take care of her." Lulu looked down the street where she grew up. Then with a slow, deliberate cadence, "I'm going to stay." Her voice slipped to a whisper. "I'm all she's got." Lulu then glanced at me, and seemed to understand that worked both ways.

Killer Birthday Cake

On the first morning of my 42nd year on this good earth, my family had unanimously forgotten to say happy birthday. I was ok with that. (It seemed my comment the night before requesting a Blue Angel flyby didn't get much traction.) Turning 42 is no big deal. It's not like turning 20, 30 or 40, let alone 50. It's more like going to the dentist and, after he hems and haws, says, "See you next year." Marking 42 is one of those nondescript milestones, unless you have a transformative epiphany, which I did, and it arrived in the guise of a birthday cake.

Like every morning, the alarm went off, we ushered through the breakfast rush with my wife managing a toddler and two elementary students, as I struggled to manage myself. Around midday my wife called to say she hadn't forgotten my birthday and that she had made a special dinner, a recipe from the Frugal Gourmet, which over the years, I'd come to learn means food that is expensive, but smells iffy.

After our dinner, a Texas/Japanese fusion potato dish, it was time for dessert. Out came my wife with a large chocolate cake made from scratch. It looked like the US Chocolate Reserve: chocolate inside, chocolate on top, chocolate on bottom, in between and chocolate within chocolate. It concealed several layers of raspberry puree, keeping the lower chocolate from reuniting with the upper chocolate…without a doubt, this was the embodiment of my dream cake. The cake I had described many times during our 11-year marriage but had never seen. This cake represented the perfect mix of flavors, bringing the fresh tart raspberries of my Pacific Northwest roots into harmonious balance with the sweet heavy chocolate. Years of Epicurean longings sang to me from its creamy core as she carried it across the kitchen.

It landed on the table with a thud of ominous authority. Quickly summoning my fork, I removed a pinch of frosting. It reminded me of the fudge my mother occasionally made when I was young. That fudge sat on the top shelf of our refrigerator, above my view; when reaching up I'd feel the velvety little cubes and read them like Braille.

Having our three young children seated at the table meant I naturally needed to assume a defensive posture to protect the cake prior to the official offering. After a short battle, in which I emerged victorious—meaning I prevented them from jabbing at the smooth exterior while still scooping another bit of frosting for myself—it was time to cut the behemoth. Lifting the first glistening wedge from the mother-round left a sharp chasm with a black hole at its center. This galactic heavyweight now sucked in light from the kitchen and commanded our full attention.

This was a man's cake. The first piece made its way to my three-year-old-daughter, where the yin/yang of the raspberry and chocolate mesmerized her until she was left motionless. Our two sons backed off a bit, knowing they were dealing with something more powerful and mystical than anything they'd ever before tried to stuff into their mouths. With no small measure of satisfaction, my wife said, "Looks kinda rich."

Once they all had a slab before them—I suspect that waiting until everyone was served felt like several lifetimes—it was time for my slice. While I judiciously measured the knife's angle of attack, I questioned my lifelong reluctance to recognize that being born is an event worthy of celebration—after all, it's just not that unique, or earned. But by the time the knife sliced to the bottom and clinked on the plate I had somehow developed an appreciation that maybe there's a legitimate reason to celebrate. Maybe all the hassle of buying presents, remembering dates/forgetting dates, sending cards, making calls, going places, playing goofy games and all the other activities surrounding birthdays could be transcended into recognizing that someone's life is worth a bit of special recognition. The fact that this change of heart occurred on *my* birthday presented a stark recognition of my self-centeredness. Luckily, the cake's mojo quickly removed any building guilt.

Exercising supreme restraint, I limited myself to three pieces. All was right in the world. It was my birthday and there I sat, full of dream cake.

Then it happened. The voices started in my head, saying things like, "Let's be friends. I'm going to be with you for a while." When my stomach started warming up a voice said, "You're looking a bit pale, maybe you should have another piece of cake." Then some other voice said, "Hey! We're out of Rolaids, you know."

Chocolate contains caffeine and I spent the night spinning like a neutron star. (About 1,000 times per second.) The next night, after dinner, I turned cautiously from the table toward the cake sitting on the counter, and approached my nemesis once again. This time I managed to limit myself to two pieces. Strangely enough, again I spent the night listening to cake voices mock me. What is going on here? Cakes used to be my friends, but this one was having its way with me.

Journal entry, dinner, day three: I ate just one piece, but with the same results.

That night as I laid in bed, heartburn fueling my thoughts, a most horrible, horrible, epiphany descended upon me—*I've reached middle age!*

When the birthday cake kicks your butt, it's nature's way of saying your life is half over. My half-time show was in full swing while I was still wandering around trying to find my seat.

So, by recognizing nature's nudge, and combining it with my mastery of mathematics, I've determined I'll live to be 84—assuming another birthday cake doesn't do me in first.

Lester's Lesson in Elocution
(To be read aloud, with vigor.)

Address the ear with a unique knock.
Tintinnabulation is how Poe
drained his blood of the mundane.

Use no inferior either
but create an atmosphere of waves
that bounce and bolt from
exultant lips.

None of Hemmingway's pale notes
his scattering of loose syllables elegant
as toads crossing a road.

Unleash a ridiculous gallop
that transforms the lands of grass
to mountains, where peaks sing
cheek-to-cheek an unrepentant psalm.
Round up the troops and ricochet among the spires.

Give way to the tongue that slays pity for
slack grammar, flat suds and soggy sandwiches.

Banish ambivalence to a language
replete with consonants willing to take a last crash
on a ragged coast before
oblivion cradles their crown.

Ghost #1: What Did the Old Man Want?

We were living in Spokane, Washington, and one morning my seven-year-old son said that the night before he'd seen a tall older man dressed in white, wearing a hat, standing in the corner of his bedroom. The man stood looking at my son, and then he was gone. My wife and I didn't think anything of it—just a child's imagination.

The following night we were sleeping and my wife and I were startled awake. I looked toward her and saw a hazy white shape, roughly the length and width of a man lying flat, floating a foot above her. The white haze, a thin cloud, was quickly rising like one side of a drawbridge from the head of the bed. In about a second it was gone.

I looked at her and practically shouted, "Did you see that?"

"Yes!" she shouted back. We didn't know yet that she had opened her eyes first and saw something much more defined than I had.

A man's low moan came from the hallway—a hopeless note full of deep regret and remorse. We looked at each other. The sound reverberated like every ghost moan in a B-movie. I thought, You've got to be kidding; this sounds so corny. But this wasn't a movie and we'd both just seen something. The long moan trailed off, but then came another. This time as loud as a person speaking at the top of their voice, sounding even more hopeless. It was hard not to feel pity. My wife and I looked at each other in silence as the long strain continued until it slowly faded. Then one more, almost a sob, as if you knew you'd be alone for eternity. This time though it wasn't as loud and it seemed to be originating from father away, maybe even traveling, leaving the house. Once it drained away, the dark once again became silent.

I realized that this entity wasn't trying to scare us with his moans and cries; he was demoralized and hopeless. Maybe ghosts aren't trying to scare the living. But since we're afraid of the unknown, it doesn't matter what they do. *It's all scary.* We'll feel fear and because of that think they're trying to scare us.

We both moved to the center of the bed and held each other. I asked what she saw. She said that about a foot above her an older man was floating, face down, staring her in the face. His wasn't a horrific or monster face, just an older man. A couple seconds after she'd opened her eyes he flew upward and away. Her voice trembled as I held her.

Neither of us believed in ghosts; that's a bunch of hokum from people with overactive imaginations, but we both knew that's exactly what we'd just seen and heard—loud and clear.

As we talked about what had just happened, we realized that telling others about this would lump us into the crowd of people with overactive imaginations, not a place either of us had ever been accused of dwelling. The whole experience made no sense to us—not who it might have been, why he was here, or why now. After a bit, just to make sure this wasn't something more terrestrial, I grabbed my bedside knife and walked through all the rooms, checked all the doors and windows, but found nothing.

Pointing to Now

Now is the blackhole of time
from which, there is no escape.
The sum of all Nows
manifests where we stand.
But Now knows no mercy
and is unconstrained by imagination.
Now rises like sharp mountains,
the immutable weight of the unmoving.
We are victims of Now's relentless pressure, yet
are still capable of climbing the clouds,
our crampons ever ready.
We prioritize and persevere.

All the while, unnoticed
the blue porcelain Buddha
sitting eternal in the garden
seems the only one who understands.

The Dialect of Silence

Clanging days can drive actions
that leave mountains of rubble and regret.
I come to know myself climbing from the wreckage.
Looking across the empty landscape
the frothy wake of my destruction leads to my feet.
Monkeys are chattering, almost in my language.
Why them? They know I hate them.
They shit everywhere in my head.

Give away the agitation.
Breathe. See myself. Still.
Monkeys wander
back into the forest
when I don't
feed them.

Mystery shrouds the stage; lights go down.
Now and only now.
I bow my head, naked,
unburdened and unknown.
Stepping out of my own way
makes room for a new creation
where a cleansing river flows
with a knowledge, but not mine.
A Camellia petal between my lips,
Its softness needs nothing,
content where it is.

Gravedigger's Requiem

"Do you have a problem being around dead bodies," the funeral director asked, as we sat at a hemlock table during a job interview. Her brown hair was styled in a bun on top of her head and her neat brown jacket and skirt were plain to the point of looking institutional.

Good question, and germane, since we were in a funeral home, in a cemetery. On the walls, shelving supported examples of grave markers and urns of marble, granite and crystal. I was interviewing to be a Family Service Counselor, one who sells funeral services either in advance of a client's death, shortly after a loved one has passed, or when they're in the final stages of a terminal progression.

Funereal arts were not something I'd given much thought to, let alone pursued as a career, but after being unemployed for nine months, with no bites, and the economy somewhere south of nothing, I wasn't feeling picky. After 25 years in cutting-edge technology maybe my model finally became obsolete, but I still needed to support a wife, three kids, two dogs, two cats, and a Japanese fighting fish named Evander Holyfield.

I thought about her dead-body question while I stared out the window into a featureless February fog. As a young man I'd worked as a commercial fisherman, and once from a smaller boat, we took on a deckhand who'd died of carbon monoxide poisoning. We didn't want to lay him on the floor and risk stepping on him, and didn't want to leave him on deck to just roll around, so we laid him on our galley table. With his lips bright red—an effect of the carbon monoxide—and a pale face, he looked like one of the pollocks we used for bait. We transferred him that afternoon to a ship with big freezers. Eating dinner that night from the table felt creepy, but we were hungry.

"Nope. I don't have a problem with dead bodies."

"Some people have a problem with that, but we get satisfaction from helping people."

Helping them what? Plan for a future they won't be part of? Support family members work through the five, or maybe it's six, stages of grief and get closure? I was just some guy off the street. Leave those things to professionals. In my previous jobs if I created an ad that didn't perform, it was disappointing, but it didn't scar anyone's psyche. Didn't leave them hopeless and pining for a hole that could never be filled. No one cried inconsolably. What if I sent a customer spiraling into a suicidal depression?

"I like helping people."

"That's good, but to do well you need to be a self-starter. The pay is commission only. But for those who really work at it the sky's the limit."

I've never taken a position that was pure commission, or ever been in sales—had always feared becoming Willy Loman, planting his garden at night. (I like growing vegetables, but have made a point of never working my gardens in the dark.) Becoming Willy scares the shit out of me.

"I'm a go-getter, always have been."

"You seem personable. When you look me in the eyes, you inspire confidence."

I'd heard that before. And like most good things anyone says about me, I tend to believe them. Maybe she was just desperate because no one else responded to her posting on Monster to work at a funeral home in a cemetery. I didn't bring squat for qualifications, but she contacted me the same day I submitted my resume.

"You can tell today is slow, no one is here, but we have three downstairs now, two services tomorrow, and one of our customers is very sick in hospice."

Downstairs? The dungeon? Movies had left me with the impression of morticians as ghoulish fiends who hid from the light. Now there were three playmates waiting? I could picture the gray skin, sunken cheeks. Not like TV— no matter how much makeup is applied, those people are still alive. When watching my father-in-law die, as the heart monitor flatlined, I could see the color drain from him. That pallor is unique to the dead. My mother in-law rested her head on his chest and wept. It was his time, maybe past his time, with all the machines hooked up. We'd pulled the plug.

"There's a lot to learn. Most people don't know of all the details, options, and laws related to burials and cremation."

That wasn't surprising, it's not like people plan funerals every day. For many, avoiding mortality is a 24x7 avocation: jogging, clicking on a birth year that shaves off some time, nonchalantly telling friends about the pulmonary embolism that was no big deal.

"You know, a few of my reps earn a good living. Did I mention that some years a few have even made six figures? I tell you the sky's the limit! Would you like the job?"

Six figures is what I'd been making for the past ten years: no commissions—no dead bodies—no downstairs—no headstones—no need for perpetual somber decorum—no suicidal spirals.

"Yes, I would. Thank you."

* * *

Julius, Randy, and Joe made up the grounds crew and I swore they knew every blade of grass by name. Julius and Randy had worked together every week for 30 years, at the same cemetery. Due to his seniority, Joe was their boss; he'd worked there 31.

Randy stood tall and lean, blue eyes, and looked as if he should have been a cowboy; his weathered skin bore witness to a life in the elements. Words weren't his strong suit, but when he spoke the room felt a little warmer.

Joe, with his slice of seniority, ran the show and spoke with confidence, understanding exactly what the team needed to do their jobs: dig a grave for a single coffin, place one coffin on top of another, remove the granite facing on a mausoleum crypt, bury a child, or mow the lawn.

Julius didn't like the gravedigger stereotype, and I don't think he was ever comfortable with seeing himself as one—seeing himself through the judging eyes of others. Gravediggers are still viewed as ghoulish fiends hunched in a muddy pit on a foggy night—wizened alcoholics at their bottom—a Frankenstein holdover.

Technically, none of them were gravediggers. Joe was the superintendent and the other two were grounds crew. But even though Julius didn't like the term, it's the only one he used: gravedigger. "We're just gravediggers, not landscape architects," he said once, after landscaping a hillside with a statue, a hedge, and a monument.

Every day, sometimes several times a day, they performed a wordless routine of digging a grave. Joe didn't wear rain pants. He sat in the Komatsu backhoe, enclosed in Plexiglas. Randy and Julius wore rain pants and denim jackets. Randy would place a plank of plywood on the grass where Joe piled the dirt. Joe dug between pins with blue flags that mark the corners. Julius would put on the final touch and shave the walls with a flat blade shovel so when they lowered the casket, it wouldn't snag. Sometimes during the rainy season the walls collapsed and dirt sloughed in so they would need to make the holes bigger than a custom fit.

Every morning the staff and grounds crew would meet in a large room used to display caskets. The funeral home trapped a separate dense atmosphere, a unique scented-candle-and-chemical smell that imprints itself during an event of high emotions. Once that smell hit, anyone returning would immediately be brought back to their first experience entering the building. Sometimes when the wind blew, I'd open the doors in back to air out the offices. The office manager told me I couldn't do that. "That lets flies in and they get into the people's noses and lay eggs. During an open casket ceremony no one wants to look at their loved one and see maggots rolling out of their nose." I never opened the doors again.

* * *

It was November, which means rain in Western Oregon, and I stood in my black overcoat, grass clippings stuck to my dress shoes and I wished I'd bought a black felt hat the day before. I'd sold a plot to a man whose mother we'd cremated. I also sold him the blue marble urn and the graveside service. The rolling hillsides around us were sculpted smooth like a green David, with the exception of a two-foot square hole about three feet deep. Julius had dug this, leaving only right angles and straight walls. Cremation burials need to be dug by hand since the backhoe is too big.

There was a card table I'd set up with a black velvet cloth draped over it. That's where the urn sat. I placed some pictures of mom on the table, some roses. Off to the side was a heap of fresh dirt that Julius covered with a section of green AstroTurf so it looked like a mound of healthy grass.

Julius and I were standing in the back as the mourners huddled under the tent awning Julius had erected. Everyone dressed in black and the women wore black pump shoes. I told the son beforehand to let the ladies know not to wear high heels; they sink into the soggy grass this time of year.

No one moved as the pastor spoke. We'd put out a few chairs, but everyone stood.

Mud streaked Julius's orange rain pants. He leaned over to me and whispered, "The Asians always dress nicely; everyone else is a mixed bag."

I whispered back, "A couple weeks ago I had people show up in flipflops."

Julius wasn't married. I could hear the chat beginning. Pretty lady: So, what do you do for a living? Julius: I'm a gravedigger. That's how he'd say it. That's how he always said it.

When the pastor began wrapping up, offering comforting words of the love that surrounds us in the hereafter, Julius began walking around the mourners toward the front. The bible closed and the pastor stepped aside.

All eyes were on Julius as he stood before the crowd, and in silence wrapped a strap deftly around the urn. It weighed about 25 pounds and with deliberate grace he lowered it into the hole. There's a special knot he used so that once the urn rested in the bottom of the hole, and the tension loosened from the strap, he would then be able to pull on one end and remove all of it. When retrieving the strap, he looked like a fisherman pulling in a net. This is a dance he'd done many times as the crowd watched. On each pull his back arched slowly. He coiled the rope, stepped to the table, and lifted a rose. Holding out his arm, he motioned toward the daughter. Softly, "Would you like to place a flower?" He then turned toward the grave.

Her movements were surrounded by a thick atmosphere that slowed every step. Bending down, she dropped the rose into the perfect hole.

He turned and pulled up a corner of the AstroTurf and sunk the flat-blade shovel into the fresh mound. Then he faced the son. The man had light tears on his cheeks.

"Would you like to place the first shovel?"

The man nodded and Julius moved toward him holding out the shovel like a sword about to be transferred at a military ceremony, offering it to the man as one last act of closure. With shaky hands he hovered the blade above the hole and turned it so the dark dirt slid off, and then handed it back. It was Julius, not the pastor, who interacted with the grieving, at least during the burial. Julius received the shovel and with thirty years of calluses motioned to the people, inviting others to take this act of closure. None stepped forward.

Monkey Business

Jack's Aquari, a pet store, stood as a fixture in the Green Lake area when I was a boy growing up in Seattle. In fact, it anchored the commercial district. Anywhere from the east side of the lake you could see Jack's huge sign, the biggest sign around, standing high atop his building, thick red letters shouting, JACK'S ACQUARI! What made the sign special, though, was the monkey, whose feet rested at the bottom of the sign but his body rose high above the shop's name, smiling with his arm up, waving at the good people below, beckoning them to come in—something like a benevolent King Kong.

Green Lake attracted kids from all around the city. A narrow dirt trail circled the lake—as opposed to the three-lane pedestrian highway that has since replaced it. We'd ride our bikes around the lake, over the roots, through the puddles, then stop and go swimming.

(One low light of Green Lake was Duck Shit Island, appropriately named by one of my friends when we rowed out to explore the tennis-court-sized territory. After he stepped from our yellow inflatable, he promptly slipped on a blanket of green slime falling face-first. "Oh, gross! This whole island is covered in duck shit. Get me off this!!!" He tried to get up but slipped again, continued slipping, falling, swearing, hollering. I had been rowing and dropped the oars weak with laughter, unable to grab them, as I drifted out.)

I'd never been in Jack's Aquari, so one day when I was at the impressionable age of 12, I decided to stroll in and visit…the cute puppies, the adorable kittens, what I assumed would be an ocean of fish, and of course, to see if he *really* had a monkey.

Stepping through the double glass doors, I entered Jack's jungle: tropical birds called from all corners, dogs barked, guinea pigs squealed, and the air hung with that wafting pet store smell of musty aquariums, wood chips and puppy poop.

My eyes darted for the monkey. No monkey. Through the aisles, still no monkey. Along the walls—monkeyless. Where's this damn monkey?

I looked up. Hanging from the ceiling in the middle of the store, swayed a cage. The monkey!

His back faced me, so I scooted to the other side of the store to see his front. But I couldn't see the little monkey's face, only the top of his head. He sat bent over with his face in his lap. I thought maybe he was asleep. So I crept closer. He wasn't asleep.

When he lifted his head to look at me, that unveiled his pink boner sticking straight up, which, coincidentally, I thought of as being the size of a pinky. A quick thought left me baffled: why we would call our smallest finger a "pinky"? Is it named after a chimp's boner? Life's too complicated. What else don't I know? Thoughts swirled.

We made eye contact. After a moment he ducked back down, wrapping his mouth around his pinkness. What? This is the cute monkey? Mr. I'm-waving-at-you-from-the-sign-so-why-don't-you-come-in-and-see-my-boner?

I stood transfixed, amazed. After a while he lifted his head again and stared at me, as if saying, "What the hell are you looking at kid? Haven't you ever seen a monkey suck his own dick?" I shook my head no, so that he'd understand we were on the same wavelength.

Who would have guessed this monkey lived here all these years and I'd never been told about him? I could only imagine a little girl asking her father what the cute little monkey was doing.

For sure, this was something my buddies needed to see. This marvel of nature could be the best surprise I'd ever come up with.

As I rode home, wind flowed through my hair, legs pumped in a happy rhythm; the tight control of balance allowed me to weave around potholes and all the while propelled forward by thoughts of the little dick-sucking monkey. That night I called Daryl, Jim and Todd, told them I had a surprise, to be at my house around noon the next day and bring their bikes.

Noon shone sunny; innocent blue sky floated above, there was a slight breeze, and a wide-open afternoon stretched ahead. "We're riding down to Green Lake," I told them. We all agreed this was a great idea.

"So what's this big secret you got?" Todd asked.

"You'll see."

"Better be good."

"Don't worry."

We hopped on our bikes and Daryl said, "Stop!" He then clipped a playing card to his bike frame so it slapped against the spokes, making him sound like a motorcycle.

When we reached Jack's, Jim looked up at the sign. "That's one big monkey. I've seen it about a million times but have never been in."

"You're bringing us here to see some crappy puppy?" Todd said. "I've seen a million puppies."

"You haven't seen this."

"Better be good."

We entered the jungle and I let them look around some. They weren't impressed.

"Hey," Daryl said. "Let's see the puppies. I can smell 'em."

"Not yet. Follow me." I took them to where I'd seen the monkey's back and pointed up like a great explorer signaling he'd found new lands. The cute little monkey—the shop's premier ambassador—remained hunched over, like the day before. "Let's go see him from the front," I casually suggested.

"I always wondered if there was a real monkey here," Todd said as we walked. "I figured there'd better one be since it's so big on the sign."

We reached our scenic viewpoint. The guy behind the counter, Jack I assumed, eyeballed us.

"Great. Is he sleeping?" Todd asked.

"Nope."

The monkey looked up, revealing his wand. Their gasps were audible. "I told you it'd be good."

Jim cupped his hand to my ear and whispered, "He's sucking his own dick."

I cupped my hand to Jim's ear. "No shit." Looking at each of my friends, I beamed like a proud father.

Todd started laughing hard enough that the counterman frowned. We stood gawking a bit more, then left, fully satisfied that Jack's was the greatest pet store ever.

Once we got outside Todd shouted, "That monkey was sucking own his dick!"

"Yeah. That's one dick-sucking monkey," I echoed. "I think that's all he does."

"Pretty good trick," Daryl said. "I wonder who taught him that?"

"Nobody taught him that you moron," Jim answered.

"Man, he must be one smart monkey." Daryl wasn't the brightest.

"So, was it worth it?"

"Hell yes," Todd said. "He was sucking his own dick!" he stated again, still processing the spectacle.

"That's one hell of a dick-sucking monkey," Jim said, as if comparing him with all the other dick-sucking monkeys he knew.

We all took a stick of gum from Jim and rode to the lake. While riding, we continually called out to each other:

"Hey, you think he's got any more of those dick-suckin' monkeys?"

"That's the dick-suckingest monkey in the world!

"You think he's for sale?"

"Dick sucking" wasn't a term we had the opportunity to use in daily conversation, so that afternoon we made up for all the wasted years of not saying it.

We rode to a swimming hole. Sun glinted from the myriad of ripples on the water and a light breeze left our world saturated with freshness. All boys were in agreement that this was a banner day. As we splashed around Daryl stopped, stood perplexed, as if looking for something. "Hey guys, when do you think they let the monkey out of his cage to play?"

The Mountain Men of New Jersey

Mountain men—we wanted to be mountain men, like Davey Crockett on TV. My friend, Will Taylor, and I were ten years old. We knew we'd developed the grit and skills to survive in the wilds of New Jersey. All we needed were the coonskin caps.

"My dad just got me a bow and arrow," Will said, as we stood in his backyard on a summer day in 1969. "It's in the garage."

"Have you shot it yet!?"

Will's backyard covered a sprawling expanse of grass that we envisioned as a perfect archery range. We sprinted toward the garage like tethered twins. Will's crew cut, plaid shirt and tan Bermuda shorts looked just like mine.

The narrow cardboard box encasing the yellow plastic bow came with its own complement of wooden arrows. "These are just like feathers!" I marveled, running my hands over the plastic vanes on the end of each arrow.

Will read from the box, "It says here they'll keep our shots straight and true."

We unrolled the paper target and gazed into its red bull's eye. Thick concentric circles, each larger one with less prestigious colors, were mere distractions for us.

"I bet I can hit it before you do," he said, striding to his father's workbench and grabbing a hammer and nail.

"What are those for?"

"We gotta stick it to a tree," Will said, shaking the target, which from the back looked suspiciously similar to the construction paper we used in school.

We walked to a thick tree on the boundary line with his neighbor's yard. I held up the target as Will pounded in the nail. The thick clank of steel on steel sounded like man's work. Once he had hammered the nail in all the way we dashed back to the other side of his yard.

"Think we should be farther away?" I asked.

"Nope. This is a good place to start practice." Will pulled and arrow from the box. Extending one hand he grabbed the point, and with his other hand he held the back, lining up the arrow just in front of his right eye. Starring down the shaft, he slowly rotated the arrow in his fingers. Like an experienced archer, he made sure the arrow lay straight. That one didn't meet his exacting standards, so he snatched another from the box. "Watch this!"

He drew back, and the shaft promptly veered away from the bow so that the blunt metal tip flopped in the air while he tried to hold the other end on the string. He angled the bow sideways, enlisting gravity to help keep the tip against the bow.

His eyes squinted to slits and I knew all he could see was the bull's eye. I could only imagine the laser-like focus he must be experiencing. He let fly. I stood watching as the arrow rode its beautiful arc into the heavens…and then into woods on the far side of his neighbor's backyard.

"We didn't need that one anyways," I said.

"Wow! That really flew!" His grin could have swallowed a grizzly bear.

It was now my turn, and after seeing Will's arrow rocket away I realized this skinny stick contained more power than I'd ever held. As I drew back, the string dug into my fingertips and I felt trepidation, responsibility, glee and some amount of competitive determination to not lose the arrow. My shot didn't sail away like Will's, but then I was sort of aiming for the target. We emptied the box of its arrows, creating a random pattern of wooden shafts protruding from the neighbor's grass.

About then Will's father stepped out onto the back patio. He stared at us. Will proudly thrust the bow above his head like an Indian brave. His father looked at the target, and noticed arrows peppering the neighbor's yard. He trotted over and quickly pulled them all up, and continued trotting as he approached us. "Damn it! Did you do this?"

I was thinking the question should have been more along the lines of "why" did we do this. It seemed obvious even to me that we were the culprits.

"Young man, I told you I have to be with you when you shoot these!" After grabbing the bow from Will's hands, his father walked away and left us unable to further exercise our manliness.

"Hey," Will's grin took on that grizzly-bear magnitude again. "I saw a dead raccoon next to the road today."

"Neat!"

"We could skin it and make a hat."

That rocketed to the best idea I'd ever heard. We'd watched *Davy Crockett* countless times and saw kids in the neighborhood with their coonskin caps. Once again, we entered the garage and Will grabbed an ancient small hatchet. He then pulled a pocketknife from his shorts. "Good thing I've got this."

We grabbed our bikes, worked up a gallop and jumped on the seats. Pumping my legs, I thought of the other kids, with their polyester coonskin caps bought from a stack at the Piggly Wiggly. They were imposters. We'd make our cap like mountain men.

After a short ride I could see a large, matted ball of fur on the road's gravel shoulder. Will reached it first and came skidding to a stop, pointing enthusiastically.

I pulled up next to him and stared down, surveying the creature, a fully mature racoon—gave it a nudge with my foot and it felt heavy. "Looks dead."

"Well yeah, dummy," Will said, wheeling his bike away from the road into some thin woods. "I don't think it was here yesterday, so it's good and fresh." He picked up the animal by a hind leg and I followed him as we walked into the trees. Will had finally become a mountain man—a coon hanging from one hand, a hatchet from the other.

Plunking the raccoon onto the ground, we studied the roadkill and discussed our next move.

Extending my hand and gingerly pinching a paw between my index finger and thumb, I said, "The hats don't have arms and legs."

"I know," Will answered, slightly annoyed. "We can start by choppin' 'em off." Will then grasped a foreleg in his palm, pulling it away from the coon's body. Raising the hatchet, he let loose with the force of a determined woodsman.

I peered over Will's shoulder, to gawk at the severed limb.

Will turned and looked up to me. "The hatchet just bounced off."

I didn't understand; Will had given it a solid whack. "Try again."

He tried. I tried. We got tired of trying. This shouldn't be so hard. After all, we'd watched *Davy Crockett*, AND *Daniel Boone*. As a test I pressed my thumb against the hatchet blade, but felt no cutting edge, more like the side of a crescent wrench. Maybe it was actually a theater prop, or something his grandfather left to his father as a joke. "This isn't very sharp."

"That's okay," Will said. "It will just look better this way." He rolled the animal onto its back. "We got to gut it now," he said with authority, and reached for his trusty blade.

I began entertaining some doubts about this venture, since we couldn't even break the skin with a hatchet. Will thrust the tiny steel into the bloated gut, and wriggling his hand back and forth got the blade to sink in. On the TV shows they never talked about the smell. With each pull of the mini-knife the blade sliced about an eighth of an inch of hide. When Will got tired, I took over. We stopped once we'd cut an opening large enough to stick in one of our heads.

Will reached in and pulled out the intestines, creating an uncoiled hose of glistening white guts. "Let me try!" I plunged my hand in and grabbed the first solid piece I could find. "This is better than shooting the bow!" Giving a good yank, the organ slipped out of my slimy grip, remaining firmly within the raccoon. "Gimme the knife." I wouldn't let a dead raccoon beat me.

We sliced and carved, saying manly phrases like "this damn thing," "show it who's boss," "I've got this." The local fly population began congregating and eventually we emptied the cavity.

"What about the head?" I asked. "The hats don't have heads."

We both looked at the head, then—looked at the hatchet. My gut pulling had emboldened me and I knelt down next to the neck. Sure, the blade was dull, but this might be an obstacle I could overcome. With several slow practice motions, I brought the blade down, but not touching the fur. Then, lifting high, I slammed down with all my might…. An orchestra of flies jumped to flight. Will was no longer interested in swinging this crescent wrench that had assume the shape of a hatchet. I made several more hearty attempts.

"It will look better with the head on," Will said. "The tail is cool."

He was right. We still had the best, most distinctive, part. I pictured myself wearing the hat as I held the bow and arrow, the tail whipping in the wind, but with my aim figured I could only hit something big, like a buffalo.

Will rubbed his head, as if sizing it. Since we'd used his hatchet and knife, unsaid rules dictated he'd get the honor of wearing the hat first. He stared for a while. My excitement was building. "You want to try it?" he asked.

I peered down and it didn't look like a cap the other boys wore. Theirs weren't wet and stinky. Our cool hat still sported its legs and head, all it's meat, and weighted about fifteen pounds. Yet again, more obstacles, but I grabbed the beast by its back legs and hoisted it up. As I held it out in front of me, peering into the crimson cavity, I realized this was a close to it as I cared to get. The yin and yang of success and failure coursed through me. Those were then overtaken by the yin and yang of having bragging rights, versus being stupid. "I don't think it will fit." I dropped the carcass and it assumed its final resting place.

By now the sun was setting, and even though we'd become bad hombres, we didn't want to stay in the woods after dark.

"We did pretty good," Will said, as he wiped his slimy hands on his shorts.

"Yeah, we did," I echoed, but suspected he felt the same hint of disappointment. Riding home in the warm dusk, even without a coonskin cap, I held my head high, but for the first time, questioned if Davy's cap was real.

Getting Boiled[F]

Last time I felt like this I was waking up in a whorehouse with a candy cane up my ass regretting how much extra that cost. This time though I'm not coming out of a blackout.

When I was a kid, I liked playing with fire. That was another one of the "signs" the shrinks talked about. They'd also ask if I liked hurting animals. But I didn't. Animals aren't spiteful. They just crap everywhere. If I step in it, it's my fault.

"Boy, sometimes I think you got shit for brains." That was one of my mom's favorite sayings, *shit for brains*. Or sometimes it was, "You haven't got the brains God gave an ant." Then the old man would show up, with a board.

There were some good times though. Once in a while my mom would buy Capn' Crunch. I'd get up while she and the old man were still passed out and load my bowl. When we had milk, and we always did when we had Captain Crunch—it was whole milk, none of that powdered bullshit—I'd pour it in until the cereal started overflowing the bowl and then I'd start chomping, smacking my lips and pretending I was a wolf. Milk squirted from the sides of my mouth, and before I was done with one bite I'd be stuffing the next one in. When there was no more cereal in the bowl I'd slurp the sweet milk—loved that feeling of the cold milk running down my throat. Then I'd load another, snarfing it up until it pushed out my cheeks and all I could hear was a marching band of crunch in my head. I've replayed that sound a million times. Funny how things like that can stick with you.

School gave me a break from my loving parents. I got the special classes. The ones kids laughed at. But it was cool. I'd get to learn at *my own pace*, they'd say. Some of those other kids in my class were freaks. They couldn't find their ass with both hands—that was one of the old man's favorite sayings. Those other kids in the class gave me a bad rep. Stigma. They stigmatized me. You can add that to the list of disorders the psychobabblers slapped on me.

But I got to reading, a lot, mostly hiding under my blankets. Teachers shoveled books my way. If it wasn't for reading, I'd be batshit crazy by now.

In high school I ran off and hooked up with a few guys. We named ourselves the Drunken Fighters. In those days we were the shit. Runnin' and gunnin'. That's what we called it, but none of us carried, not then. We were just kids trying to act tough. We lived up to our name though. By then I couldn't stand anyone laying a finger on me, and I made sure nobody fucked with us.

The boys didn't want to call me Jimmy. They said it sounded like a little kid's name. A crowbar showed them I wasn't some little kid. After that they called me Jimmy, and that's all I'd let 'em call me. No more dumb-ass or fuckwad. None of those guys could find their ass with both hands, so I made myself president. Hell, I'd never led anything before. I got us working cars—loved how my heart pounded when the alarms went off.

"Now what the hell did you do!?" my mom would scream over the phone. I don't know why I called her for bail each time. By then the old man was dead. Served him right to die drunk. At least I have that over him.

Punk this, punk that, everyone called me a punk. Everyone except the punks I hung with. We got a few more members. That's when Katie showed up. She was pretty then. A tight little ass and a sharp tongue. She didn't take lip from nobody.

Even then we didn't talk much, but we got a place. Being at the end of the runways made it hard to keep the boy asleep.

When he was a baby all he did was bawl. Drove her crazy. He had the colic, so I'd just leave. That way I couldn't hit him. Swore to myself I'd never lay a hand on him. That's funny—the thing I'm most proud of is something I never did.

We were pretty small-time: smash-and-grabs at liquor stores, dealing some dope, boosting car parts. I thought about pimping, but Katie was getting fat.

After a while I told her I'd keep in touch. Gave her money when I could. Got to see Little Jimmy sometimes. I taught him a thing or two. Nothing sketchy, good stuff, like how to shine-on a mouthy salesman, or when instructions didn't make sense, then adapt, modify.

I signed him up for Little League one year, and even went to a game. They let him pitch a couple innings. He struck out three batters and came running off the field and jumped into my arms. We held each other like there was no tomorrow. I started tearing up. Afterwards we went out and had burgers, fries, shakes—the whole shebang. Best day of my life. Period.

But he's not here today.

Eventually runnin' and gunnin' became real. The Drunken Fighters all carried. Pistols are a lot harder to aim than in the movies. I couldn't hit the broad side of a barn. None of us could. They were mostly for looks. We were kinda like family, but eventually John Law caught up with most of us. I haven't heard boo from any of them in years.

Of course burning down that house is what did it. Sure, it was no secret there was bad blood between us, but those motherfuckers finally pissed me off so bad I was seeing red. I didn't know there were kids asleep in there and that's the God's truth. I still have nightmares. During the trial I swore I didn't remember anything; that's also the truth.

All I do remember is kicking things off with a half-gallon of Southern Gentleman and some Pabst. Cheap whiskey mixes great with cheap beer, makes them both taste better. That's called a boilermaker, and man, I'd get boiled.

Some guys say they wouldn't change anything, even if they could. Damn straight I would. First thing I'd change would be to get born different. I guess you could say my slide began early on. Can't change the past though. And that's a piss-ant excuse anyway.

That's about it. Nothing special. I didn't become an astronaut cowboy.

I never liked the way footsteps echo in these halls, sounds hollow, like ghosts walking. Anyways, looks like the chaplain's here with my Cap'n Crunch.

How to Watch a Horror Movie

Alone.
No other voice to validate you exist.
A big empty house, but a hotel room will do.
Doubt yourself.

That face: a few teeth,
the rest smashed out.
Gray lips. She approaches, slowly floating,
wearing a nightgown of spider webs.
Getting closer, she grins: embers for eyes.
Blue veins cross her cracked cheeks.
Cold stale breath, a lunge, and she
locks on for a bottomless kiss,
her hot tongue descends into your bowels
while you gasp for air.

Turn off the TV.
Go to bed. Slide your hands between
the cool sheets, swipe wide.
Make sure no one is hiding there.

Turn out the lights.
Stare at the blank ceiling.
Now, the horror begins.

The Wall^F

A shiny black tail slipped beneath a crack between the floor and the wall in the far corner of what had been Tom's bedroom. He saw it, or at least thought he saw it. (Maybe it was one of the hallucinations.) A quick motion captured in his periphery. Odd, what was it? Tom had been wandering around the vacant house and was feeling more and more amped-up for adventure, so he stepped in the room to take a closer look.

At twenty-two, he'd dropped any childish fears of the dark or being alone, even as the only one at his family's remote summer home in Montana. The place had been in the family for generations and sure, coming from a wealthy family was nice and they always expected him to behave with certain decorum, but his generation was being told to turn on, tune in, and drop out. It was the Sexual Revolution baby! And he had some plans to let things flow. Things best left unknown to the family. When alone there, he knew he could do whatever he wanted. He never told friends, but he thought of this place as his thrill palace.

He stood tall and skinny, with straight stringy hair, as he unsheathed his hunting knife and stuck out his tongue. Holding the knife up broadside, he flipped the tip of his tongue like a French tickler on the dark metal. He could taste the acrid iron, a lot like blood.

To get the evening going, he'd dropped two hits of Purple Microdot LSD and they had been coming on. He was fantasizing, thinking what he might do to get a little freaky-deaky that night. Never can tell what might happen, he thought, whose paths may cross, two legs/four legs, and the 'cid helps get the groove going. Various colors and sparkling points lit up his vision as the acid continued to take hold—his private light show as he entered into this investigation awaiting him in the corner of the room.

It was early fall and frost lasted most of the day, but that was the only way he could have the place to himself, especially since his dad was in the middle of selling it and the deal was going to close in a week. Without any furniture and no electricity, the grand old house stood as a dank empty shell, but Tom still wanted to come one last time. One last blowout maybe. This was the land where he knew how to cover his tracks. He walked across the bare wood floor holding a flashlight. The narrow cone of light that projected in front of him made him feel like an explorer questing for novel pleasures across earth's mysterious reaches, which is exactly what he had come seeking.

As he walked toward the corner, he thought again that the tail he'd seen may have been a hallucination. Not likely though. He'd done enough acid to separate the drug-induced visions from reality. This was a snake's slender black tail, about a foot long, disappearing into the seam between the baseboard molding and the floor.

Kneeling down he could see the gap where the snake had retreated. Tom hadn't noticed that before, but rationalized he'd never dropped on his knees with his head in this corner—of course he hadn't noticed it before. The gap remained black, even when he shone his light right into it. Streamers of neon colors began to form around the hole, reminding him of lines on a topographic map. They pulsed and wiggled, whizzing into the blackness of the gap.

Tom stuck his fingertips into the vibrating pool of black where the radiant lines of red, green, and blue shot into the stillness. He could see the colors streaking down his fingers into the gap, like little pixies he thought, showing him the way. While he watched his fingers elongate and move deeper into the wall, he brought in his other hand and let it flow with the pixies. So easy.

There must be plenty of room. He tucked his head down between his arms like a diver and lights exploded before him and surrounded him. Blinding rays of light raced past him, streaming to a distant future where they disappeared in a sea of black, beyond his sight. The dark quickly began getting cold. His flashlight was gone.

A dim red glow began to appear above him in the distance. His arms were raised straight above overhead and looking up between his hands he could see the orb getting brighter. As the crimson light shone, more details emerged. Looking up a narrow chute, he could see his front and back were sandwiched between what seemed sheets of plywood. The sheet on his back appeared smooth as he looked down its length. The sheet pressing against his face had nail tips randomly protruding from it. Each of his arms were confined by what appeared to be long 2x4s. When this hallucination didn't continue transforming into something else, Tom's heart started racing, thinking he was about to experience a bad trip. He'd had one before where hundreds of images of an old girlfriend's face, drawn in blood, moved across all the walls, as if they were lined up on multiple conveyor belts.

The glow intensified and Tom felt his hands pulled up toward it. His face began to slowly skid across the wood as his chest compressed, causing him to expel any remaining oxygen in his lungs. Tom heard cracking and felt stabbing pains while his ribs folded in. The pull intensified and his shoulders popped as they dislocated. He strained to scream out in agony but even his jaw remained anchored closed under the pressure.

More exposed nail tips became clear as he was being drawn toward them. The red glow crackled like a cinder until hot snapping filled Tom's head, as the nails worked their magic and left ragged red furrows along his body. Nails penetrated into his cheeks, chest, thighs, everywhere, each of them gouging along his skin until he came to a stop.

Unable to inhale, he panicked and every muscle spasmed but nothing moved. With his arms stuck above his head and body compressed into a spaced only several inches thick, the red glow raced away like the other lights, leaving Tom unable to see anything, in fridged silence.

* * *

"Oh, James. This place is way better than even in the pictures!"

The voice from outside the wall jolted Tom's attention after months of isolation—his ridged body now a desiccated husk.

"You were definitely right that we should wait until spring to come out here." James lowered his voice, thinking no one could hear, "Winter here is colder than a witch's tit."

Two young boys came running in between them, as Helen held three-year-old Olivia in her arms. "Oh, you two. This is not a gymnasium!" She turned to Olivia, with a happy coo, "You are soooo lucky, little one."

"You've got that right," James said as he leaned in to Olivia's face, giving her gentle taps on the nose. "If mom didn't want to risk having three boys, we wouldn't have adopted you." Olivia responded with a sly smile.

The movers followed right behind the family and the house that had been locked tight for six freezing months burst to life.

"Hey, it kinda smells in here. Like, like…rotting: stinky, sour dishtowel, rotting rats." Billy always liked being precise.

"Thank you for your assessment, Mr. Nose," James answered. "It's definitely musty, but once we get a little air through here that will clear out fine."

"Hey dad, can we go fishing now?" James Jr. was eleven and ready for some of the outdoor adventures the family had been talking about during the previous winter.

"Son," James tossed up his hands, "I have no idea where anything is. We're here for the next three months, and for plenty of summers after that." He clasped the boy by the shoulders. "I'm excited too. Don't worry, we'll get in plenty of fishing. How about you start by trying to find the rods?"

They had arrived from Manhattan and this was to be their new family summer retreat. Some might call it a compound. A nice quiet place, not ostentatious. No need.

Olivia began to squirm so Helen put her down. She stood for a moment: long brown hair, apple dumpling cheeks and wearing her red polka dot dress. Then she bolted down the hall squealing with joy and disappeared into one of the rooms. Everything was working as planned and the entire family knew they were in for a wonderful summer. James and Helen held a long embrace as they took a moment to recognize they were building their family and watching their dreams materialize in real time. "I love you so much, honey," Helen gave him a quick kiss. "But I've got to track down Olivia."

When Helen turned to look down the hall, she saw Olivia standing in a doorway, holding a flashlight.

"I want this room."

"Where did you get that, sweetie?" Helen asked as she approached. Olivia pointed to the far corner. "Well, we had planned on this being your new room, so I guess that's your new flashlight. The previous owners must have left it." Olivia smiled and hugged the light, holding it close to her chest while rocking it like a baby.

Moving is always a stressful day for everyone and Helen could see it was beginning to take its toll on little Olivia, plus her nap time was coming up. Helen directed the movers to bring in Oliva's bedroom furniture and she set up the bedroom in time for the child's nap. The two of them sat on Olivia's bed as Helen stroked the girl's hair, relaxing her. Once Olivia laid back and rested her head on the pillow, Helen got up and closed the curtains. "I'm going to close the door honey. It's noisy out there but we're all right here." Olivia gave a sleepy, self-satisfied smile, and closed her eyes while still hugging her new flashlight.

* * *

"Hello Tom."

Hearing someone address him made him want to jump up, at least flinch, but nothing. He remained frozen, arms over his head with nails stuck in his dried skin. He recognized the voice, but only vaguely. This wasn't one of the voices coming from outside the wall. This voice was in his head, but he heard it, loud and clear.

"How have you been? Enjoying yourself? Enjoying the serpent? He's enjoyed you."

Tom's mind raced: Who is she? Where is she? Can she get me out of here?

"Do you know who I am?"

"No, but you sound fam…"

"NO?!" she screamed. "No, you don't know who I am, do you?"

Now Tom knew who she was. What's happening? Frozen and alone for six months set a baseline for a new state of existence. He was still alive, yet not, but this voice introduced something incomprehensible. "You're dead."

"Obviously not, shithead."

Tom could see this getting ultra-ugly, even without any idea of what ugly may entail. Several years ago, he had come across a lone woman hiking during one of his stays at the house while he was zooming on acid. He told her about the energies of the universe and she chuckled. How dare she? When his face suddenly hardened, the woman took in a sharp gasp. That made her breasts heave up. Tom's focus changed.

"I sent the serpent," she said. "Once I told him about you, he was more than happy to pay a visit."

"Olivia, that's your name. Olivia. I remember from your driver's license."

"When did you look at that? It was definitely after you stabbed me. You didn't have time for any reading before that. Was it after you cut off my hands? Is that when you looked at it? Did you know I was only in high school? You don't even know why I was hiking by myself."

"I tho…"

"Shut-up! I was there because my dad had just passed away and we used to hike on that trail. We'd spend hours talking about life and she showed me so many things. I was full of grief and gratitude. Then you came along. Do you have any idea at all what you've done to my mother? She was a good woman, but I was all she had left."

"I'm sorry. I didn't me…"

"SHUT UP! You don't know what sorry is. But you're going to learn. And you did mean it. You meant everything that day and that's why this worked out so well. I'm getting a second chance. But for you, as long as this wall stands, your soul stays stuck in that corpse. You're going to pay for my mother's suffering, and I want you to know that you will never equal what she is living through."

Tom wanted to weep, but had nothing for tears. This isolation, squeezed into his vertical coffin, could easily last decades. Many times he'd heard his father and grandfather say how well-built the home was. Solid as a rock. "Nothing like today's cookie cutter houses," his grandfather would add. All of his muscles ached as they cried out for movement and his broken bones rang with pain. But what he hated almost as much as the loneliness, was that the nails never stopped feeling like fresh wounds.

"I've been with this child since her beginning, but she's soon going to forget about that life I had, and all the ones before. She's here to help this family be whole. She'll be her own person and never know what her eternal soul has been through before now. That's the grace we get."

"Get me out of here!" he begged. "I'm sorry! I'll do anything. Anything!"

Olivia rolled over and kicked her legs against her blue blanket dotted with smiling yellow moons. She opened her eyes and wondered what a dumb flashlight was doing in her bed. As she made her way to the bedroom door, she dropped the flashlight in her garbage and walked into the bustling home.

When she saw her father, she ran up to him and hugged his legs. "Daddy, time to go hike!"

Ghost #2: From Atheist to Saint

Six months before she came to our home, she came to my wife in a dream. I'm not Catholic and my wife's not Catholic. Yet saints are the product of the Catholic Church. This visitation remains puzzling.

In the middle of the night I awoke for no particular reason—I was a much lighter sleeper than my wife, Sheila—and saw a fuzzy white form in the general shape and size of a person in a cloak. Its back was turned to me and the head and shoulders were obvious but below that offered little detail. It began walking/floating away toward an open door, then stopped.

I was up on my elbow, looking at this hazy white thing, still less than ten feet away. Then it turned its head toward me. As it turned, I could see a woman's face, and she looked right at me. We held our gaze. Her eyes were as white as her skin, and I felt they were kind, while her facial features appeared smooth. Her overall expression appeared neutral, looking at me as if reading a newspaper. As it dawned on me that I was looking at a ghost, I strained to see more details, knowing that this doesn't happen often and wouldn't last long. Her face was clear, but everything behind her cheekbones was a featureless white fog. It seemed a line, ruler-straight, ran down the side of her face, hiding what was farther back and revealing only her eyes, nose and mouth. I felt frustrated, since there should have been more detail considering how close she was. I expected to see hair, ears, or something.

After a moment she slowly turned and resumed her steady pace away. I felt no fear watching her and she was in no hurry. Having reluctantly accepted that ghosts were real after that first encounter, this second one almost seemed normal, like seeing an eagle—rare, but no need to freak out.

She walked along a wall, heading toward an open door. The door was already open 90 degrees from the wall, and I assumed when the figure reached the door she'd turn left and walk through the doorway. Instead, she just kept walking straight along the wall, right into the swung-open door. As she passed through the door her outline became even more clear. Once she was half way through, her outline began to shrink and draw in as she moved forward, until it looked like a circle quickly closing and reduced to a point, then vanished as she disappeared behind the door.

Still no fear. Someone who came and left. I reviewed the whole thing in my mind several times and it dawned on me maybe I was dreaming. I could think of nothing else to do than give my forearm a pinch. No, I was definitely awake. My heart wasn't pounding. It was the middle of the night and I felt tired, so I decided there was no need to wake my wife. When I told her in the morning, I explained the ghost looked like a woman in a cloak and when she turned back to look at me the hood of the cloak obscured part of her face.

* * *

About six months before that night my wife woke up in the early morning agitated and inspired. She'd had a violent dream that was so vivid she wanted to conduct some research on it. Over our thirty-three-year marriage this is the only dream that caused her to followed-up with real-world investigation.

Her dream images were quick cuts of soldiers hitting helpless people with the butts of their rifles, there were broken bodies lying on the ground, and in all of the scenes everything was drenched in shades of crimson. People were screaming in different languages, but one phrase rang above them all, and was repeated multiple times. I hate to say it, but I don't recall the exact phrase and I can't ask my wife, since she has passed. However, as Sheila researched the phrase online, her efforts repeatedly led directly to one woman—Edith Stein. Neither my wife nor I had ever heard of this person.

As Sheila learned more, it seemed the images and sounds in her unusually vivid dream held some level of connection with Edith Stein, as she was a nun who had died in a Nazi concentration camp, and it was easy to see how the dream images could relate to that.

* * *

One evening several days after the ghost's appearance, we were talking about the mystery of the ghost and what was up with the cloak. We looked at each other at the same moment and both had a "eureka" expression in our eyes. It wasn't a cloak, but a nun's habit, and we connected it back to Sheila's dream. We looked up a picture of Edith Stein and it was virtually identical to what I saw when she turned to look at me. The habit explained her obscured hair and body.

Edith Stein was a German-Jewish philosopher born in 1891. She was born a Jew, became disenchanted with religion and adopted atheism but continued to contemplate her spirituality, and then converted to Christianity to become a Discalced Carmelite nun called Sister Teresia Benedicta a Cruce (Blessed of the Cross). Eventually, she was canonized as a saint by Pope John Paul II; a Jewish/Catholic saint—talk about unique. Because she was born a Jew, as the Nazis increased their persecution of the Jews in the late 1930's, she was reassigned to a convent in the Netherlands for safety. Even with that she didn't think she'd survive the war and began preparing herself for life in a concentration camp, remaining outside enduring cold and hunger. She even wrote a letter offering herself as a sacrifice of atonement for true peace should she be taken.

Eventually the Nazis ordered the arrest of all Jewish converts who had previously been spared. The SS arrested her on August 2, 1942. She was shipped to Amersfoort and Westerbork concentration camps before being deported to Auschwitz. It's likely that on August 9, only seven days after her arrest, the Nazis murdered her in a gas chamber. The church even offered an escape plan, but she refused it, saying she couldn't abandon her brothers and sisters.

For this she was beatified as a martyr, but to receive full canonization, and sainthood, she needed more than that. She needed a miracle.

Even without a miracle, Edith Stein's life was amazing: she worked as a nurse, earned a PhD in philosophy, wrote prolifically, became a Jewish nun, has had plays written about her, schools named after her, and movies made of her. There is even an International Association for the Study of the Philosophy of Edith Stein (IASPES).

The miracle for her canonization is the curing of two-year-old Benedicta McCarthy, who had gotten into some acetaminophen and swallowed 19 times the lethal dose. She lay in a coma, with total kidney failure, her liver was swollen five times its normal size and she was suffering from a serious infection. Doctors wanted to conduct a liver transplant but no doners were available. They predicted she would die. (Little Benedicta was named after

Sister Teresia Benedicta a Cruce, who had been beatified the year Benedicta was born. They also shared the same birthday.)

The young girl's father, Emmanuel Charles McCarthy, a priest of the Melkite Greek Catholic Church[1], immediately called his sister to begin a prayer chain, with more people calling more people to pray for Benedicta. Knowing Benedicta was named after Sister Teresia Benedicta a Cruce/Edith Stein, she seemed the natural one to pray to for intercession. Within days, Benedicta came out of the coma, her kidneys began functioning well and her liver shrunk back to normal size. She walked out of the Massachusetts General Hospital in Boston. Dr. Ronald Kleinman, MD, treated Benedicta. He was the Physician-in-Chief at Mass General Hospital for Children. Dr. Kleinman testified about her recovery to a Church tribunal, stating: "I did not expect her to recover from this.... Things went from bad to bad to worse to worse...I was willing to say that it was miraculous."

Regarding the nature of this ghost, we can manufacture connections that may consist of only wishes. Here, however, there are enough dots for me to believe the spirit of Saint Teresia Benedicta of the Cross came to our bedroom intentionally from some connection with my wife, and as an unplanned occurrence, she and I stared into each other's eyes.

Beyond that, I don't know what to make of this. Sheila and I could find no Earthly connection as to why she'd have that powerful dream and why I'd ever see a Saint, as a spirit, in our bedroom. Maybe someday more will be revealed.

---

1. McCarthy is a priest in the Eastern Rite of the Catholic Church, a branch that allows a married man to become ordained.

Edith Stein/Saint Teresia Benedicta of the Cross

Rushing the Sun

Freedom to wake
raises me in the wet dark.
The cat stares, quietly
searching for morning, while
a ship's clock chimes.

My sail of confidence, trimmed to run,
waits with me in the dim.
Every dream a snaking wake that dissipates
like an old man's memory.

Rain, direct to its destination,
falls with a certainty
even faith can't change.

Plans wander through options,
to touch and smell,
searching for a meal.
Ready to embark
once the door of dawn opens.

Bells chime again, while
the cat and I bask in the
futility of rushing the sun.

America the Beautiful

None of Hawaii's junkyards are popular tourist destinations, but I found one anyway—at the end of the Honolulu Airport runways. When I reached paradise, after scratching together enough to buy a one-way plane ticket from Seattle, I knew I wouldn't be living large but never thought that after a month I'd be kneeling in greasy sand, looking down at my black hands, knuckles red with gouges, stripping engines from dilapidated wrecks. I didn't just find a junkyard; I was working in one.

Abandoned cars doubled as apartments for stray dogs. Dogs were everywhere: mean, mangy, just skin over ribs. I learned to look inside each car before opening any doors. They didn't like surprises.

As a twenty-year-old this was good adventure. I'd taken a break from school but was learning junkyard etiquette: shut-up, keep working, don't whine. It was worth it though since I got to live on a leaky sailboat that was even closer to the runways. My hair was long and sun-bleached, skin well-tanned. I looked like a surfer bum but had never been near a surfboard. Surf was for washing up at the end of the day; its foam was my bubble bath.

One day I squirmed underneath a '65 Chevy Impala to un-bolt its rear differential. Only my shoes were sticking out from under the car. I heard something and turned to see Mr. Yaseen's black boots kicking sand as he walked toward me. Mr. Yaseen was a fat guy with a thick black mustache and thick black hair. He'd leased a blistering wedge of Sand Island that held his acre of cars stacked five high. He was being evicted and had me scavenging anything of value. At the end of each day he paid me in cash.

"Hey, Steve!"

"What?" He was practically standing on my shoes.

"Come here."

Wriggling through that sand from under the car was like plowing through gritty peanut butter. Mr. Yaseen stood next to a short brown guy. He was skinny and the veins on his arms bulged like blue rivers through a muddy delta. He was a bit younger than me and his T-shirt and shorts were more worn and frayed than mine. And mine looked like hell.

"This is Thanh, fresh off the boat this week. You work with him. Show him the tools."

Thanh could see my hands were gummed with grease and sand, but he stuck his hand out to shake. As we shook I gave Thanh my best sarcastic smile. "It looks like today's your lucky day." His head bobbed in eager agreement. That creeped me out.

Mr. Yaseen walked away through a canyon of butchered cars.

"So, where you from?"

"Vietnam."

It was 1979 and Saigon had been captured by the northern Communists only four years before; no one from Vietnam just sauntered out of the country and into the United States. I asked how he got here.

"Refugee." He worked to form each word, "Five years in Thailand."

Then it dawned on me—Boat People. He's one of the Boat People. Originally, they fled South Vietnam as the north made advances. For a while they were in the news. As they made their way along the Gulf of Thailand in overcrowded boats, Cambodian pirates hunted them: they killed the men and raped the women; they'd steal everything; people starved and plenty of boats sank. A family's life saving might send just one person.

Some people made it to Thailand and that's where Thanh's waiting began, along with his English lessons. Eventually the United States welcomed over 400,000 of these people as immigrants.

This became the first time I'd met a real, *real*, refugee. I didn't know what to say and just told him we could work together. We spent our time cannibalizing anything we could reach—cutting cables, yanking engines, pulling out radiators as fast as we could. Fuel and fluids leaked and sprayed on us. The sun's fever evaporated everything but didn't lift the penetrating reek of gasoline from our skin.

Four hours after Thanh had started working we had our heads stuck in an engine compartment when I asked him what it was like. I stopped turning my wrench to quiet the clicking of its ratchet. "I mean, in the camp, what was it like?"

He cranked his head up to look at me. "Three camps: bad, dirty, not food enough."

"Pretty bad?"

"Yeah, pretty bad."

I took a crate of transmissions away on a forklift and when I came back Thanh was leaning into an engine compartment so far he was upside down.

Mr. Yaseen walked up to Thanh's butt and yelled, "Hurry up! We don't got all day!"

I leaned in and started working on the other side of the engine. Once Yaseen left I said, "He's a butthead."

"Yeah, butthead."

I wondered what other important words I should teach him.

By late afternoon we were both wearing grease up to our elbows and our faces were sheened with sweat. While we were taking a drink of water I decided to show him some American culture and thrust my right arm up, index finger pointed to the sky, cocked my hips as provocatively as a junkyard worker can—I was channeling John Travolta from *Saturday Night Fever*—and crowed, "This ain't no disco...You know? Disco?" I swung out some dance moves.

He danced a little jig and sang out, "His hien no disco."

I had no idea what he thought that phrase meant but we started laughing. As he raised his arm and posed with a finger pointed to the sky, the bones of his elbow bulged from under his skin.

A memory snapped close my laugher. There had been a news story a couple of years earlier about a young Vietnamese boy who'd been on a boat that was sunk by pirates. The boy had survived and remained afloat by hanging on to two bloated corpses.

When Thanh stopped laughing, he stood smiling.

The next day there were a bunch of alternators in the front seat of a car and they needed wires removed and to be boxed up. We laid a piece of plywood over the sand and sat on it. As we were finishing, I screwed up the courage to ask the one question that had been on my mind all day. "Where's your family?"

Thanh lowered his hand and drew a shape in the sand that looked like a fat hook. Then he flipped his finger, forming a hard straight line across the middle. It was Vietnam. He still saw the border dividing the north and south. He thrust his index finger deep into the southern sand. "Communists kill my father. My mother."

Thanh kept facing the sand, inhaling sharp short breaths. Tears fell like dark bombs on his country.

He lifted his hand, then struck down, pounding his fist into the sand, widening the hole his finger had made. Pounding. Pounding. Twisting his fist back and forth in the small crater. "They kill my brother, my sisters."

He punched the sand again and again. "I hate the communists. I hate them!" He lifted his head. Tears had eroded channels through a layer of dust that covered his face. He sat defiant, without shame, looking me in the eyes. "I want Freedom."

We sat in silence and I held his stare. His fist still pushed into the sand. I could only think of one thing to say, "Welcome home."

The One-Second War

A Dark Bomb in the Digital Age

This piece is a long-form journalism article I had hoped to include in this book. All of my beta readers said it didn't belong here and they were right. (In writing parlance, deleting something like this is referred to as "killing your darlings.") But I couldn't totally let it go; it's too important.

Few civilians understand that society's increasing reliance on digital technologies, and electricity in general, has created a situation in which a singular nuclear weapon detonation can now destroy huge swaths of infrastructure—up to the size of entire continents. What originally was considered a byproduct of a nuclear blast has now become the weapon's most potential destructive force. This byproduct is called an electromagnetic pulse (EMP).

In 2001 the US Congress created a commission to assess the threat of an EMP attack. The commission issued a report estimating that within one year of a single garden-variety nuclear detonation used to maximize EMP impact, up to 90 percent of all Americans would be dead—more than 300 million people. Every building would be left standing, yet modern society would be leveled. For the United States, this means from the Atlantic to the Pacific, and from Canada to Mexico. Again, this is from just *one nuclear bomb*.

This article is long, terrifying, and true. If you're up for it, you can find it here, http://halyardpress.com/emp.

When Angels Speak

My friend Barry is disabled. He wasn't always that way, but 40 years after coming out of a six-week coma induced by a random drunk driver, he's rebuilt his life. If you were to look at him, you'd see a doddering old man with a cane that you'd hope wouldn't come up and start talking to you, but somehow, you'd be pretty sure he would, and you'd get to worry about what level of discomfort you're about to experience.

He doesn't really *like* speaking with strangers, but at times he overcomes his hesitancy and resistance to awkward situations and speaks up. One of those instances happened on a BART train running through Oakland. He was sitting a bit hunched over with his cane and a woman in her 30s sat down next to him. She appeared clean, pleasant, and they sat in silence. After a few minutes a voice in Berry's head told him to say hello to the woman.

No. That's weird. She'll probably think I'm some old creep hitting on her, he thought. The voice again said, "Say hello to her." Barry now recognized the little voice. He calls it God.

Berry turned, extended his hand, and said, "I'm Berry."

The woman burst into tears.

Once she recomposed herself, they started talking. Whether it was intuition, or the voice, or something else, Berry suspected the woman had drug and alcohol problems. He confided to her that he was in AA and that he had had drug problems, but he was now sober and happy.

They continued talking and as Berry's stop approached, the woman told him that she had boarded the train specifically so she could go home to kill herself, but now she didn't want to. Berry stood up, told the woman that God loved her, and he stepped off the train.

Let Fly
The archer's release

A tensioned twig springs,
unleashing the power of compressed history.

The moment gains momentum,
pushing against gravity like a finger
on a painting. Throwing itself
forward, the canvas implodes
folds and vanishes.

Unveiling a blood covered moon
above a blue peak
with an amber figure ascending
on a coyote's swirled howl.

Cookies Are Hell

One cold day, in a surprise attack, a kindly white-haired matron from my church deployed a new weapon on the Afghan battlefield.

Our church in Spokane, Washington, about the size of a fancy garage, sat in the middle of an empty field. In the winter snow its whitewash provided perfect camouflage. All that stood out were the black window panes.

The only warm place was the kitchen. So it didn't surprise anyone when Betty, the leader of the Sage Hens bible study group, suggested one afternoon that we bake cookies. After a flurry of flour and sugar many a cookie was had by all. In our cookie-satiated happiness, we decided our troops in Afghanistan could use the same boost and that we'd send them some. Everyone agreed that was a great idea.

In fact, Betty stood before the congregation and asked everyone to bake cookies at home and bring them in so we could send even more. "Winters are also plenty cold in Kabul," she reminded us. It was understood that these couldn't be just ordinary cookies; these had to be cookies that could carry the flavor of home across the world.

After the service in the fellowship hall, as people stood drinking coffee, they talked of their cookie plans:

"Oatmeal raisin…no, no, I'm adding cranberries also."

"I've got some bars I haven't made in years, graham crackers, chocolate, caramel, coconut," a middle-aged lady mentioned, with her hair in a neat brown bun. Then in a whisper, with her hand to a neighbor's ear, "One man called them O-bars because they're so good they're orgasmic."

"Chocolate chip with walnuts, extra walnuts!"

"Snicker-doodles aren't fancy, but I'll bet they remind someone of home."

"Mine uses sixteen ingredients," a jovial woman said, as children swarmed around her like ducklings. "They bake into chewy little mountains."

Betty proclaimed proudly, "I found a recipe that's guaranteed not to spoil." She rotated her body back and forth indicating she was about to address all of those within earshot. "Found it on the web, and it says they will last for up to a year without refrigeration." That sounded practical.

My three kids banded together and suggested to the pastor that the following Sunday, if people wanted to bring a few extra cookies, then the congregation could sample what the troops would be eating.

While my wife baked peanut butter with chocolate chip cookies, my kids offered unrelenting assistance:

Hey mom we'll clean the beaters.
Hey mom this batter is sticking to my fingers.
Hey mom can we do this tomorrow?
Hey mom can the dogs have one?
Hey mom let's make enough for all the soldiers.
Hey mom you can't lick the spoon.

By the end of the afternoon we'd managed to package five dozen for the troops, eat two dozen, and reserved another dozen for church the next day, which the kids had christened "Cookie Sunday."

It looked like Christmas before the service as armloads of boxes with cookies began stacking up in the fellowship hall as people dropped them off before heading into the sanctuary. This didn't escape any of the kids circling a long table where a kaleidoscope of cookies awaited, but these snacks were for after the service, more importantly, after Sunday School.

I taught the second and third graders on this fortuitous day. In exasperation I finally said, "If I bring in a clown with his hair on fire followed by an army of cuddly bunnies, would you stop talking about cookies? Please!" The incredulity in the air was palpable. We finally discussed what types of cookies Jesus might like. And decided he'd like the ones we were sending.

Class ended and the Spirit overcame the children as they ran from the classroom so they could gaze upon the table heavily laden with a cornucopia of cookies—The Promised Land.

The first hint of trouble came when a cherub stuffed his maw with one of Betty's cookies that will never spoil and proceeded to howl, "YUCK," and let the plaster-white mush from his mouth drop to the floor.

Betty hadn't yet arrived, so some investigation was in order.

If the other golden-brown cookies were rows of Californians sunbathing, then Betty's were a column of pale subterranean trolls. My wife picked one up, held it to her nose.

"Nothing, this doesn't smell like anything." She gently placed a dainty corner of the cookie between her front teeth and bit. Unfortunately, her teeth weren't making a dent. She inserted the slab along the side of her mouth, the way a cabbie might chew on a cigar, and gave it a chomp.

With the grace of a debutante, she used a napkin where she discretely deposited the bite. After watching two people spit out the cookie, I was dying to taste one.

I grabbed one of the petrified pucks and after several hearty chomps, the bite became a glob of elementary-school paper mâché in my mouth. Betty came strolling in all smiles. Displaying manly fortitude, I swallowed the doughy mass. At this point, seeing one of her partially eaten cookies in my hand, she strode toward me.

"Well, what do you think?"

"What's in them?

"Oh," she smiled benevolently as she prepared to relay the simplicity of it all to someone equally simple in the ways of baking. "They're water, flour, salt and anise."

That would make them elementary-school paper mâché with anise.

"The recipe was used as far back as the Civil War, when there was no refrigeration."

"So, they're like heirloom cookies," I choked out.

Happy voices swelled in the room, punctuated with an occasional "yuck!," creating a background din that let me drift in thought.

I pictured a soldier sitting on the dusty ground, his back against a mud-brick wall, looking out to a barren Afghan plain. I could see him opening the cardboard box of cookies. Maybe smiling and thinking of his wife's cookies, maybe a sweetheart's, maybe his mom's.

He chomps on his first cookie, gazing to the sky. As he continues chewing, puzzlement crosses his face. Then his chewing slows, and finally, stops. He has not yet swallowed anything. In fact, the dumpling of dough seems to be expanding in his mouth at an alarming rate. His battle-hardened reactions allow him to spit out the gob before it blows up his head. He thinks it might be fun to bring them back to his squad and use them in a practical joke, but instead, he leaves them for the Taliban.

Vacations Are Supposed to Be Adventures

Vacations are supposed to be adventures; that thought was my rock in a sea of mosquitoes. My family and I were leaving for five days of boat camping on an island in the Columbia River where we'd find an isolated beach and set-up camp. We had done this the previous year and the experience was priceless—two miles of solitary white sandy beach, sunny days, fishing, swimming, good food and campfires.

As with any vacation the anticipation and excitement built, until we arrived at our boat, a twenty-four-foot cabin cruiser. When I turned the key, rather than the engine roaring to life, my stomach did. The engine cranked over but wouldn't start. I tried all the tricks I knew but stopped before completely draining the batteries. Our boat was moored next to a shipyard and I found a mechanic. While I drove to and from parts stores, the family worked at entertaining themselves for five hours before we got the engine started. My wife, two teenage sons and a ten-year-old daughter devised multiple ways to sweat less while simultaneously trying to stop our two dogs from pooping all over the dock every chance they could.

If we raced, we could find a campsite before dark. So we blasted off and with all the camping gear, food, water, dogs, kids, wife and me, it was amazing how slowly the boat traveled over the next several hours.

We did make it to camp before dark. The current was moving right along so we anchored in a slower back-eddy near some old pilings. The next step was to row our dinghy to shore, bringing a line, and use the line to pull the boat in close enough to unload the supplies. We'd also pound a piece of rebar into the sand and tie off to it as a permanent shore anchor. The tension between the bow and shore anchors would keep us steady.

My sons, Mattson and Pierce, lowered our dinghy and got the rope ready. Matt sat down and happened to row away just as Pierce was stepping in. It took Pierce about one second to generate a giant splash. My wife immediately became convinced that Pierce, who had been on a swim team, was now drowning and started throwing lifejackets at him. And while she hurried to save him from a certain watery death—which would have been a bummer on the first day of vacation—I noticed that the eddy current was now carrying us toward the jagged pilings.

Pierce climbed back on the swim step, and they rowed off, sitting in our bathtub-sized dinghy yelling at each other. Once they reached shore, it became evident they'd forgotten to bring the rebar anchor, which was the main reason for their trip…debate ensued, while we drifted toward the pilings with broken timbers jutting out at head level. I launched into an apoplectic dance and enthusiastically informed the boys they needed to start pulling the rope.

Once secured, we unloaded the boat like Amazon explorers, wading through the water carrying the supplies that would sustain us for the next five days. We setup several tents just back from the soft sand and built a wall from driftwood that blocked the wind and became our kitchen.

The boys lit a campfire and we were ready for a hearty dinner. Our menu called for guacamole cheeseburgers, potato salad, veggies and dessert. When I went to the coolers it seemed I couldn't find any of the delicious ingredients. So I just called my wife over and asked her to grab the food, since she had packed it and knew where it was. After a few minutes she came over, but not with packages of hamburger and guacamole, rather, with an expression of blank terror. Not a good sign.

She was now reasonably certain that all of the food for our dinners and other miscellaneous goodies were sitting in the refrigerator at home. Returning home would mean six hours round-trip running on the river, plus a couple more hours getting from the marina to the refrigerator—that would burn a whole day. We were only spending four nights and decided we had enough non-dinner food…but it would be an adventure. On the bright side, our dogs had plenty of kibble.

So we ate a breakfast-dinner and discussed our food deficit. Inside of me the glee of the hunter/killer re-awakened and I was now in survival mode, primed to secure whatever source of sustenance I could. Otherwise, for the rest of the trip my family would be forced to eat sandwiches, chips, watermelon and other unsuitable dinner fare. It was go-time.

The boys, at the primitive ages of 13 and 14, had had the same re-awakening and we were all ready to tap into our inner cavemen. Luckily, we had brought a pellet gun for target shooting and they suggested we feast on starlings. With about 500 pellets I didn't think we had enough ammo for that approach. What we needed were fish, and to get them we needed fresh bait. We now knew our marching orders for the next morning.

Morning opened with a crystal sunrise, seagulls calling in the distance and a gentle breeze rippling the waters. The warm sandy beach stretched out in each direction and there were no other people in sight.

There are many species of fish in the river and they all like fresh bait. In our altered consciousness, the seagulls were looking more and more like flying bait balls. Our primal maladjustments allowed us to remain constantly vigilant for any opportunity to shoot a seagull. After some stealthy time, lurking behind a row of poplar trees, the golden opportunity presented itself and we snapped into action. I pulled the trigger and the bird fell to the sand. Pierce ran and grabbed the flapping ball of feathers. He wrestled with it valiantly, squeezed it here and there, but the creature continued flapping and making unhappy noises. I reached in and popped its neck for a quick dispatch. Success was ours! (Yes, every seagull in the United States is protected under a federal law. I now consider myself a hardened criminal, stand back.)

Unfortunately, this all occurred right in front of my daughter—the one who wanted to be a marine biologist so she can help the animals.

As her sobs filled the campsite, the boys and I continued our business of survival. Luckily, she was so upset and disgusted that she ran into her tent, where she stayed until the next morning. In an act of solidarity, and with equal disgust, my wife joined her—a true *Men are from Mars, Women Are from Venus* moment. We were now free to slice the bird into nice bite-sized chunks, in a hidden location.

We casted here, trolled there, spoke kindly to the fish, chanted and did a fish dance, but ended up catching nothing and discussed if the right move would have been to eat the seagull. We did, however, have to swear to my wife and daughter that no additional seagulls would be harmed in the making of our vacation.

The next morning found us still smarting a bit, but a hearty breakfast of eggs and potato chips did the trick, and the entire family felt the holiday mood again. The wind blew gently and a pair of ospreys hovered over us. One dove into the river with talons extended and came out clutching a nice trout. The bird provided a beautiful display of grace by a skilled predator. (Unlike our effort with the chopped-up gull.) We walked down the beach, climbed sand cliffs, ate handfuls of juicy blackberries, identified birds and their nests, and played football in the water. Each of us had a chance to shine.

After lunch, the wind had changed and we noticed more sand in the air. Riding in with the sand were mosquitoes. Not a problem, modern repellent works great and we'd brought several kinds, until I looked for them. Somewhere, probably safe at home, sat our bug juice.

My wife became a mosquito delicacy. So much so that they avoided the rest of us like bloodless stones. We have pictures of my wife's legs looking like a minefield with all the mines exploding at once. To this day the only thing she remembers about the trip are the mosquitoes, the itching, and the glorious satisfaction of mass murdering the little buggers; when the mosquitoes were around she'd morph into Charles Manson and go on a killing rampage, a bit scary, but quite entertaining.

Later that night, with her guitar around the campfire, she'd morph into Joni Mitchell, or even Neil Young. We all sang, tossed wood on the fire, and roasted marshmallows.

Our bucolic privacy was interrupted the next day when a boat pulled up about 30 yards away from our camp. Never mind a mile of unhabituated beach stretched out on either side with great campsites; these people appeared determined to camp right next to us. Their boom box blared distorted mechanical fart music, and it seemed they'd been drinking a bit more than a bit. At first we thought they were partying rednecks, but then noticed they all had shaved heads. Our new beach mates were partying redneck neo-Nazis. My boys said they'd make good bait, but we didn't go that route. As the day progressed their boat came and went bringing more shaved heads every hour. Our idyllic private beach had become a redneck-neo-Nazi-tourist-hotspot. They ignored us, which was our preference, but we kept an eye on them. As night came it appeared they were involved in a competition to see who could throw a baby the highest. (I'll swear on a Bible I'm not making this up.) As far as we could tell, someone caught the infant each time.

They left the next morning and we continued to play, took in some target practice (my daughter bested her brothers and myself), ate eggs and pub mix three times a day, until it was time to pack up and return to the dinners awaiting us in the fridge.

Ed Zeppelin

At dinner, after listening to one of my stories,
a child asked, "who's Ed Zeppelin?"
Even then I couldn't tell if aging
was a lost art or nouveau fad.
Just as boomers "discovered" sex,
we're now the first to age.

Every amoebae knows the drill
and we always knew it,
but couldn't confess to
our averageness.

The story you are about to read is true, only the names have been changed to protect the idiots.

Go. Go Faster!

"Go. Go faster! We can make it," Stev shouted as he sat reclining in a La-Z-Boy. His overstuffed chair was plunked in the back of an open truck bed along with two other La-Z-Boy chairs, containing two other lazy boys. The boys had been on the road a couple hours, headed to a bluegrass festival, but they needed a break for some unknown reason and decided to go off-roading. Stev was soon to learn he had dramatically overestimated the capabilities of the well-used 1969 Chevy pickup.

They entered the Skagit Flats and maybe they were heading for a dike, maybe it was just a pile of dirt, but at Stev's urging they were convinced this mound was no obstacle to their juggernaut of bluegrass-fueled enthusiasm, let alone their Liebfraumilch-fueled ridiculousness. However, sane people would tell you there was absolutely no hope this jalopy would do anything but plow into the embankment like it's a concrete wall.

The guys in the cab were wearing seatbelts. The guys facing backwards with their chairs against the cab just sank back into the chairs. Since his chair faced forward, Stev launched, sailing him straight into Jef's face. Jef was shaken but not damaged, although Stev had opened two gashes, one above his right eye and one below it. The bluegrass run turned into an ER run.

Three hours and thirteen stitches later, Stev walked away from the ER to a far corner of the hospital parking lot where the boys sat parked in the shade. Even though they'd been waiting for hours, they hadn't left festival mode.

A nurse had given Stev two aspirin but all he could feel were the pulsing jolts of pain around his right eye, which was swollen closed and featured a multitude of colors. There was also the matter of the blowout bone fracture behind his eye. This wasn't the plan.

The plan was to put three overstuffed recliners in the back of Mar's 1969 Chevy pickup. That way, while breezing down I-5, they could wave to the other drivers who thought they were crazy. Two guys sat in the cab and all of them were headed to the Darrington Bluegrass Festival in the foothills of the Cascade Mountains. The day awaited full of music and mountains.

Through his one good eye Stev could see it had been a pass-around-the-wine-and-bullshit afternoon for the boys; for them the festival would have been better, but not much.

"What the fuck?"

"What the fuck, fuck?" Jef answered from his recliner in the truck bed.

"So are all of you drunk?"

"Maybe," Mar said. "But I sure as hell am." The other three agreed.

Stev eyeballed the jolly troop. There was Jef, Mar, Berni and Da. All were single guys in their early twenties, just out for fun. Life was good, but they felt it was great.

Jef motioned with a wine bottle toward Stev. "You gotta drive, man." He swung his head and glazed at his friend. "Whoa...you look like shit. Goddamn man, you can only see through one eye."

"I hadn't noticed." Stev wasn't sure what to expect when seeing the boys, but a truck full of drunks wasn't it. Had he given the matter actual thought, though, this, in fact, was the only thing he could have expected.

The sun was about to drop below the horizon and they still had a couple of hours before reaching Seattle. The drive would be a bear but Stev was relieved he wouldn't be going through life with a fat scar splitting his eyebrow and continuing on his cheek. The road became a blurry mess when his good eye watered up.

In the rearview mirror Stev couldn't see anything. Two recliners blocked the rear window. Occasionally he could hear muffled yells from the back, but there was no need to stop; it was dark and they could pee into the empty wine bottles.

TWO ACTS OF THREE

ACT ONE

Ditty About Gadding

I gad about the countryside.
We gather to gad some more.
So glad we are to gad with ease,
across your ballroom floor.
Where men turn back, we dare to see,
while gadding along so gleefully.
By chance you spy our gadding group,
fear not
gone with the wind are we.
Too bad.
So sad.
Gotta gad.
See you next time.
Maybe.

Stallions

We didn't know. We knew we didn't know. We didn't care that we didn't know. And that was fine.

Those sunny mountain days at a grassy airstrip, playing Frisbee. The VW bus blaring bluegrass from the open doors.

Flying over the dandelions, landing only when we could run no more.

Muscles rippling under the sun: those horses, those stallions, us. And if we had a care, it was that we had no cares.

No shirts, no shoes—we didn't need any service.

Rain and mud welcomed us with open arms.

Passing around Liebfraumilch. No need to dirty a glass. We were cork liberators!

Maybe we did know, but not fully, how crystalline youth is. How smooth and sharp and clear.

How being twenty-two, single, without a job and living in the mountains meant never reflecting—no time. We raced toward the world with hikes and harmonicas, swimming, and nonstop friends who wanted a taste of the freedom we gorged on every day.

When the wine was emptied, we'd head back to the cabin on the riverbank. No electricity, but the running water never stopped. The potbelly stove we cooked on. The loft for lovemaking.

Night meant you couldn't see your hand six inches from your face. I'd become small enough to fit in a matchbox, and sleep there until the sun returned my size.

We posed for a pic in that airfield—its faded orange windsock the only sign that the expanse was ever intended for planes—some ragtag Frisbee brothers that had to share a toothbrush because they'd spent their money on sweet white wine.

ACT TWO

Not Everyone Knows Their Favorite Word

Soporific: that's mine.
The vowels slide
like lips over my lips.
Its whipped cream of
syllables light and airy,
with a dream-inducing onomatopoeia.

I met soporific as my
wife read *Peter Rabbit* aloud.
Mrs. Tiggy-Winkle was feeling
soporific. I nodded, asking what that meant.
(I wasn't not going to know a word Mrs. Tiggy-Winkle knew.)

Two months married and she read me books
which had imprinted her, commencing with Beatrix Potter.
Lying in our first bed,
she curled her soft fox tail
around my shoulders.

I didn't need to understand
another corporate platitude,
bow to every paradigm shift,
so I can hit the ground running
to maximize efficiency,
while my neck-tie is
tied too tight.

Only her voice cradling my ears.
"Soporific means you're tired."

I nodded again. She kept reading
and I kept listening
to her heart-beat, as my head
rode the swells on the
slow ocean of her breathing.
Soporific whispered, as I slept
in my bride's arms.

Like Water

We understand ourselves flowing.
The downhill mountain rush
propels our course.
Multitudes of rapids scour banks
along the same stream.

The understood life pours in, and
we assume the shapes of our vessels.

A friend's voice
smooth as the molten bend
at the top of a waterfall,
beckons us over the edge.

Wide and gentle,
gravity takes its ease, and torrents
subside in rolling eddies,
leading to amniotic oceans pulsing under the sun.
While in the clouds, our children
are waiting to reign.

My Alligators

Serpentine bathrobe belts snake
behind squirming crawlers.
My two alligators prowl the living room carpet.
Their toothy grins snap at goldfish crackers.
The larger beast saves the smaller from "bad guys."
Today's menagerie bares its teeth.
Chubby arms maul my ankles
in this warm swamp.

Tiny Histories

Today is the state championship.
Tomorrow I'll paint a room.
Milestones of unrelated magnitude
mark the loss of eras.

Win or lose, they'll live
to never play as a team again.

Crayoned pictures and plastic trophies
embellish a small bookcase.
When the paint dries,
they won't go back up.

Chunks of memories break away, floating,
carried on irretrievable currents.
Attaching nostalgia doesn't secure them.

I'll store my daughter's dollhouse in the attic
where our intertwined histories
forever tug like distant kites.

She Doesn't Eat Peanut Butter

It never occurred to me that unicorns
Poop rainbows. This makes sense.
Not eating peanut butter,
That doesn't make sense.

Tonight she returned from the store
Chips, hummus and all.
I asked about the peanut butter, my touchstone.
She said I must tell her
When I need more.

Where Paths Diverge

In a pre-dawn parking lot,
I reached up, placed my palms on
my son's temples and
kissed his forehead.

With his crew he drove away.
Going to fight his first wildfires.
Adventure, becoming part of something.
His time begins.

That afternoon he called from the Phoenix airport,
to wish me happy Father's Day,
and apologize for not remembering earlier.
I'd forgotten too.

Footsteps are not
always for following,
but a guide, to show
where paths diverge.

Hummingbirds

Half me, but stronger
and wiser.
Delicate jets, not these.
They kite in, each a unique beauty.
Bold spirits create lift;
arrows melt in their wake.
Years become a flash,
each frozen moment
to hold with a hot grip,
nothing can take away those.
Burned in memory,
after they light out.

Family Tree

We are the pulp
that forms each page of history.
Brambles tangle us in chaotic mosaics.
Warmth ignites a blitzkrieg of blossoms.

When crosscut, course shards
pattern our droughts,
weaving survival from blanched splinters.
Rings reveal
endurance, marking
syncopated seasons
we rise through.

Jumbled roots draw amber lines
mapping the past,
connecting all tribes
to outstretched leaves
where each green flicker
beckons for light.

No Shade from the Cold

Pathology is an afflicted word.
Reminds me of psychopath.
That bleeding.
The staff got her into surgery,
the next day.
Afterward, the oncologist spoke, with empathy.
"In thirty-five years, I've only seen this once.
If you want to do things, travel, visit people,
do them now."

> The next day we'd dig out our bucket list.
> What was on it again?
> No travel plans, or people to visit.
> Just the penciled layout for our next home
> titled, Future Grandkid Magnet.

The doctor walked out.
I closed the exam-room door
and in her strength
she held me as I sobbed.

# # #

When We Weren't Fishing

"I can't hear you. I'd better put on my glasses."

That's what Gramps said as we lay in our beds in the dark, talking, after a cold sunny day of trout fishing. It was just the two of us, along with that faint smoky smell that sanctifies old log cabins. Both mattresses sagged like sway-back horses, making them extra cozy, each covered under several quilts. The year was 1969 and I was eleven.

He'd rented a small cabin outside of Twisp, Washington—a place where years later I'd bow hunt deer. The fire in the wood stove sent flickers across the room, the only light. As the wind blew outside, he asked if I'd liked the dinner we'd eaten at the Twisp Diner. "I didn't think you were going to finish that big steak."

"My tummy kind of hurts."

He laughed—heard me just fine, must have put on his glasses. "Where would you like to go tomorrow?"

"What was that lake we were at last year? Where all the fish were big and we caught our limits?"

"Spectacle Lake. Now there was a bang-up day. It's about an hour from here."

"Can we rent a boat and I'll row us across the lake?"

"I'd expect nothing less."

Earlier that day we were on a shoreline at the base of a steep embankment. Our footsteps had left deep imprints in the loose dirt. He took a puff on his Chesterfield, gazed up, backtracking where we had wandered down. "When I was a young man I could run up those banks like nobody's business." His buddy, Roscoe, once told me that Gramps could also run the bases like nobody's business.

As we lay in those slack beds, cradled under heavy warmth, he told me that for years he'd taken horses into the back country to hunt elk—pitching camp with some buddies and spending a week. On one trip they were driving on a mountain road that clung to a steep hillside. A wheel on the horse trailer lost traction and slipped over the edge. It began a slow sink as the dirt gave way and it continued to pull the truck backwards. Gramps was in the passenger seat. "I tell you what, if we didn't move quick, I wouldn't be here and neither would you." He and the driver bailed out just before the whole rig toppled off the edge. In a moment, the truck, the trailer, and three horses lay dead a hundred feet below them.

"They're amazing animals, elk." Slow silence. A log in the fire crackled. "The last time I went hunting, I had a huge bull right in my sights. He was so magnificent…. I just couldn't pull the trigger."

As an adult, I can picture him, kneeling in the snow, rifle at his shoulder, still, conflicted. How long did he stay like that? How long did it take to make the decision that something he'd loved for decades was over? Maybe it felt like a death in the family, maybe a birth.

"We'll need to get more marshmallows tomorrow," I said. "We ran out today." We used marshmallows to float our bait off the bottom. I'd eaten our remaining ones that afternoon.

"Sure, we can get marshmallows. We can get some steelhead eggs also. I think those trout like steelhead more than I do."

"Not more than I do."

Gramps was also a steelhead fisherman. He had built a plywood boat that he called his *Skagit River Scow*. Its boxy wheelhouse could squeeze in two people. The splintered decks had long acted as an altar where steelhead met their maker.

"Grandpa, how'd you become a fireman?" As a little boy I'd always thought the top three jobs for a man were fireman, astronaut, and cowboy.

"It started when the fire chief gave me a call and asked me to come down to the station. I was just a minor league ball-player and couldn't figure out why he wanted to see me." Gramps said the chief sat in a large office, behind a dark oak desk in a stout chair of authority. "I was scared and figured I must be in big trouble, but didn't know for what. So when he asked if I wanted to join the department I was so relieved I just said 'yes' as fast as I could!" He laughed, but I was shocked. That's not the way I'd pictured it. A couple decades later, he was the one sitting in the chief's chair.

My mother once told me when she was a girl, Gramps came home from work and cried for a long time. Earlier that day he'd carried a dead child from a burning building.

"What do you want to be when you grow up?"

I knew what I wanted but was afraid to tell my family. They wouldn't approve, especially my father. "I want to be a writer."

"A writer? What sort of things are you going to write?"

"I'm not sure—stories I guess."

"You'll be good at that. After all, you like to talk."

"Mostly to you." But he already knew that.

He reached across the narrow space that separated our beds and gave mine a pat. "How about we get some shut-eye? We've got fish to catch tomorrow."

Thunder Dogs
(an observation)

Dogs have many noble traits, like barking at annoying kids, peeing on the neighbor's lawn, and keeping you awake at night so they can sleep while you're at work. In parts of the world dogs are revered as brave saviors, paths to the spirit world, and dinner. However, one thing all dogs seem to share, regardless of their social status, is an abiding fear of thunder.

In other aspects of their lives, dogs are fearless. They'll charge armed robbers, stand up to a bear, and even trot out right in front of a speeding truck. They're furry superheroes! But one clap of thunder and it takes a SWAT team of canine psychiatrists to coax them out from under a bed.

If you live in an area with few thunderstorms, then your dog's therapy bills are probably within reason. We once lived in Texas, where there are frequent and dandy thunderstorms. All of the neighborhood dogs were on federal disability for PTSD, Post Traumatic Stressed Dog.

Of course, the severity of the dogs' reaction to thunder is directly proportional to how deep asleep *you* are. During the day a huge thunder clap will cause little reaction, unless you're napping. At night, reactions can range from running under the bed and howling, to jumping into the bed and spraying pee everywhere. Either way, you are alerted that the tensile strength of their courage has softened a smidge.

Dogs that remain outside don't have these types of reactions. They're accustomed to being in the elements and know instinctively how to deal with thunder. They simply go into their shelters, remain quiet, and quiver until their fur falls out.

Large size is no shield against this fear. In fact, the bigger the dog, the bigger the fear, which makes them seem even more pathetic. To see a Doberman seeking refuge under the legs of a three-year-old isn't a pretty sight. As the first boom subsides, these normally brave beasts universally start to channel the spirit of Don Knotts. (History lesson: He was the bugged-eyed, slump-shouldered, skinny little goober who starred in the movies, *The Ghost & Mr. Chicken*, *The Reluctant Astronaut*, *The Shakiest Gun in the West*, and other classics. One of American cinema's great anti-heroes, and a heck of a dog channeler.)

What to do about all this? Of course, there is the obvious solution of moving to a place where there is no thunder, like the moon. Or you could grab your pooch and insert little doggie earplugs. Then, while the thunder is crashing all around, you can sit peacefully in the emergency room while your hand is being stitched up.

Aside from that, these enthusiastic souls may not be our smartest friends (and for some not the dumbest), but once the thunder subsides, they will crawl out from hiding with tails wagging. And when they see that you've survived, they'll be overcome with emotion and urinate with joy.

Love-Hate Relationship[F]

The only woman he ever loved married the only man he ever hated. Jason's last happy memory of Carmen remains enshrined with her driving a Jeep Wrangler out of the Sedona mountains, top down, blond hair under a baseball cap. Her tan face radiated enthusiasm, with a smile that penetrated to his heart. That night she flew back to Manhattan; Jason returned to Palo Alto. That was about a year ago.

They'd met at Princeton as juniors. Three years later, she was the only graduate student in the Physics Department who didn't sport a penis. Not that she couldn't get one if she wanted. Jason had noticed her only about a million times, like everyone else: professors, classmates, waiters, jocks, campus security. After working together on several lab projects, he managed to work through his intimidation—asked her if she'd like to go canoeing on the Delaware. Jason saw her as half beauty, half brains, and half glorious grace; even as a physics major, he didn't care whether that added up. The world holds more than we can perceive, and some of that beautiful mystery peeked from Carmen's eyes.

On that initial date they talked about physics (something they both said was strange and that they must both be geeks), nature, their families, aspirations…then the kiss. Over the following months her presence gave him confidence, like looking into a mirror and seeing a reflection of the man he'd imagined he be someday. If she ever felt threatened, she'd turn to Jason as her sanctuary. Then they graduated with their master's degrees.

As PhD candidates, Carmen was accepted at NYU. Jason, at Stanford.

Over the past year Jason had learned that absence doesn't make the heart grow fonder; absence makes the heart grow agitated. After multiple unanswered texts, he called her. "I just found out my cousin is getting married in the Bronx. That's a good enough excuse for me to fly back to New York."

"You need an excuse?"

"I need to rationalize." As a grad student cash was not an intimate companion. Money flowed only one way, out. The Physics Department never intended his stipend to support a transcontinental romance. "Family will be there, so maybe I can get my father to help out," he said to Carmen. His father came through, and Jason's airfare didn't eat into his food budget.

Normally he wouldn't fly across the country for a cousin's wedding. He'd spent time with his cousins, aunts, uncles, second cousins, great aunts, and great uncles, but never became close with any of them. Like people who attend church on Christmas and Easter, there was an element of obligation, rather than a passion. Seeing Carmen fueled the passion.

At the reception she smiled politely as he introduced her around. She was polite enough to Jason, asked him how his flight had been, how he had been doing.

Eventually they sat down and Jason introduced Carmen to his father, Jim. "Well Carmen," Jim said, as the three of them sat at a round table covered with a white tablecloth, "it's nice to finally meet you. You've become a bit of a celebrity with your *Times* article about gender inequality in the sciences."

"I was just telling it straight." She'd been complimented and criticized for her article published the month before. Her provocative, non-politically correct premise was that when surveying a large population, men are better wired to develop advanced math. "I wasn't the only woman in my graduating class because others didn't want to graduate." She looked Jim in the eyes. "They just couldn't hack it. I was there, watched it every day." She leaned closer in and took a swig of her wine. "They just didn't have the horsepower."

Jim smiled at his son. "Looks like we have a Ferrari here, a very special one."

Jason's attention snapped back to the conversation when he heard words directed at him. "Yep." He took a moment to study his hands. "Runs on premium, I guess." After her cancer, he missed his mother more at times like these.

That night Jason was staying in a hotel, but Carmen had to drive back to Manhattan. "Something came up."

Growing up in Manhattan, Jason had only one real friend, and their relationship sprang from competition. Jason's earliest memory of school consists of watching Billy swing higher, so Jason pumped harder. They tied, understanding how hard the other had worked. In class they compared grades, jockeying back and forth for the A+: for the smile, bragging rights, and knowing the rights would shift before too long. Individually they stood out some, but together they were better than the next ten. The Two Musketeers didn't need a third. Once the boys launched their growth spurts in middle school Bill maintained the advantage, remaining a couple inches taller, providing an opportunity to lord this over Jason, both of them knowing this wasn't something any amount of effort could equalize.

Whenever Bill came over to the brownstone to visit Jason, Jim would complement him, saying how big and strong he was getting. Spending time in the gym increased Jason's strength but didn't make him any taller, and didn't stop his father complimenting Bill. In high school when the boys played football, Bill had grown to 6' 1" and Jason was 5' 9". Bill made the starting squad; Jason made the practice squad. Football had always been his father's favorite sport and he watched every game.

He knew his father was disappointed in his performance. His father was also 6' 1" and had retained his athletic build and energy. Throughout Jason's childhood his father made many comments about "being over six foot." That seemed to be the bar to cross. Jason assumed he would, like his father, without trying.

Whenever he saw Bill at the games, Jim had developed a routine. He'd ask him how tall he was now, but asked it a different way each time: have you tacked on another inch? what's your altitude now? are those shirtsleeves a bit short? Bill always indulged him with elaborate answers on the minutia of his training routine, aches and pains, or any other important stuff guys 6' 1" would talk about.

Archery, there was a sport where size didn't matter, and Jason had always been attracted to precision. No need for football, so he quit. The archery coach said he was a natural: balance, strength, concentration. As he won competitions his father and Bill watched, when they were available, but spent most of their time talking to each other. In Jason's senior year, the football team won state. The team got a special assembly and players were high-fived throughout the halls. When Jason won state, he got a special mention in the school paper. Bill told Jason archery was cool, but that nobody really cares. "No shit, Sherlock."

After high school graduation, Bill attended New York University, as he put it, "gracing the Polytechnic Institute," only half-joking. Many of his classes were a few blocks from where the boys grew up. Since Bill remained local, he and Jim met every month or two for dinners.

Several weeks after the cousin's wedding, Jim texted Carmen and invited her to one of the dinners with Bill. He felt that having Carmen there with Bill would keep the conversation moving, since they all shared history with Jason, almost like having him there. Carmen laughed at the funny stories Bill told about growing up with Jason. The men learned Carmen shares their taste for good scotch. During the evening they drank, ate great food and traded stories—Jim covered the tab.

Then the two of them started seeing each other more. More dinners, more talk about school, Jason, aspirations. They both told Jason that they were seeing each other on occasion. Not mentioning those things would have been impossible, disingenuous. They felt obligated.

"God Jason, he's so much like you!" The phone felt cold. "And you're so far away." He knew what was coming. He'd been expecting it, unsuccessfully trying to drown his suspicion. Keeping his mind on school helped, but his thoughts always drifted toward Carmen, calculating the inevitable, but not like this—not with this humiliation. Being taller, his commanding presence, the sophistication of Manhattan. What would his mother think of this? The equation made sense, but the answer became intolerable. After only nine months, they married.

A whirlwind. They were infatuated, not grounded, not constructing the years he and Carmen had built. The deceit, the treachery, knowing the pain their marriage would cause him, every day they were together, every night. There were a million—twelve million—other fucking people to pick from in the city. How could they possibly choose each other?

This was intentional. A chance to rub his face in failure, to confirm ultimate dominance. This was an intentional arrow aimed at him—killing him if it could. Destroy his ability to concentrate on the intricacies of graduate-level physics: sap his horsepower, cause him to take some crappy job teaching high-school math, land some crappy weak wife—someone who'd produce kids that weren't over six foot, not on the football team.

He got on a plane.

Walking up to their door, he thought of how he'd kissed each bullet the night before. Now, all that remained was who would answer and fall first, Carmen, or his father.

Ghost #3: Oh! You Pretty Things

This ghost story is difficult to tell, because it's the most out-of-the-blue and makes me sound the nuttiest.

Middle of the night I wake up. Lying on my back I look to the left where there's a picture window with horizontal blinds lowered. Standing still in front of the blinds, crisp white, no hazy mist, stood a man who I immediately realized was a ghost. I could see the lines in his face so clearly my first thought was "He was a smoker in life."

Elegant describes him, or maybe *languid*, graceful with a relaxed disinterest. He was there for something, but also for something else. I was able to watch him for a while and study him closely, because he didn't see me. He was a tall, lean man with one hand raised in front of his face, extending one finger, that lifted one slat of the blinds, so that as he cocked his head to the side, he could look through the window. He stood still, just looking out the window. The silken hand with the extended index finger remained stationary, with the subtle grace of a Michelangelo.

His well-pressed suit jacket fit impeccably and the creases down the front of his trousers ran razor sharp. His hair was moused-up in a stylish fashion, especially for an older man, but he didn't have that trying-too-hard look. Since this was now my third ghost, I appreciated his clear appearance, even though he consisted only of shades of white. As I studied him, time allowed for more thoughts and his concreteness of appearance made me begin to think there's a *man* in my room. I knew he was a ghost but that flash of a thought—that in the middle of the night there's an unknown corporeal man standing close to me—caused me to gasp. In the blink of that gasp he disappeared. I've thought many times how this might have unfolded had I just calmly remembered he was a ghost, and said hello.

Although unusual, I didn't give this a lot of introspection. The experience seemed barren: a few unconnected facts that didn't interact with any part of my life, as far as I could tell. The next day it hit me, the strange part, when trying to describe to my wife what he looked like. The similarities here are more than passing, especially his face. This fit perfectly.

I'm hesitant to say this because—well, because you'll see; the ghost looked like David Bowie, looked a lot like David Bowie in his later years: the face, the suit, the pose, the hair, the demeanor. This incident occurred about two years after he'd passed.

Was it Bowie? I have no idea. But if it was, he's just as elegant as ever.

Note: I was going to include a photo of Bowie wearing a white suit, in which he looked nearly identical to what I saw. However, the photographer required $3,500 for me to use it in this book. You can view it for free at https://andina.pe/ingles /noticia-perus-mario-testino-pays-tribute-to-david-bowie-593773.aspx).

Mary's Desk[F]

Mary likes the phone; it's big, black, and powerful, and she controls it. Sometimes the lights for all six lines blink. Music plays when she sticks people on hold. Not the type of music she would listen to, when she remembered listening to music. If she wanted, she could wear a headset, but that isn't often; once the metal band grips her head it makes her feel like a robot.

Back when she sat at the front desk more people talked to her. But now, with the lobby remodel behind schedule, she sits in an alcove in the back corner. How can a remodel take four months? Are all the workers drunk?

All of the execs enter through Mary's lobby, and twenty-two years ago, when she started here, the CEO himself said to her, "You're the voice of the company. When people call, you're the first impression they get. You're like St. Peter at the gate." A huge responsibility.

Every morning she puts on her face: a good layer of pale foundation (even when her skin was young it deserved a solid foundation), a red slick over her thick lips (her best feature, they might as well standout), green eyeliner, and a tight watchman's cap of straight black hair ending in bangs just below her earlobes. Over the years her breasts had been getting heavier—cleavage looks nice, but it's easy to cross over into too much of a good thing.

Even though nobody calls to talk with *her*, she talks with everybody. Plenty of times callers commented on how politely she spoke, the bounce in her voice—like a cup of cheer. Some even made a point to tell her supervisor.

She built her desk around the phone, always had. Pictures give wide berth to its squad car of blinking lights. Pencils in an old coffee mug stay clear of the cord. Note pads earn the closest audience.

Charlotte's middle-school picture sits propped next to the empty in-box. Mary knows she's old enough to be a grandmother, but hadn't expected it to happen so soon. The blessed event—that's what people called it—surprised everyone. She knows Charlotte and the baby will be staying at home, probably for a few years. Seems the only blessing was Charlotte's having the baby in the summer, between her junior and senior years.

Ted peers from behind cloudy picture frame glass on the far side of Mary's desk—dark hair and smiling, wearing that powder-blue jacket with the wide lapels. They look wider each year.

The last time it'd been this slow was about five years ago, the day Reagan was shot. Maybe something bad has happened. She hates not knowing.

Today there'd been only three calls since eight, and soon it would be lunch, which she rarely takes. If she were gone, calls would route to the executive assistants, and they have better things to do. They'd come to expect no miscellaneous interruptions. These days, hidden behind the lobby, she can eat at her desk.

Before, she'd stare through the big glass doors. Things changed out there, cars in the parking lot, sun, rain. Now she stares at an oversized plaque with the red corporate logo and a small painting of ducks in a marsh.

Ted. He'd been in a funk. Not his fault he said—no one wants to hire a bald salesman. He told her his looks don't give off the right image, not enough hungry predator. Years ago he'd worked on some house projects. But now, the front door bangs on the jamb, the upstairs sink barely drains and stinks. A little paint wouldn't hurt anything. It wouldn't kill him to vacuum once in a while, get off his butt. When was the last time he mowed the damn back yard?

The phone rings: relief. This caller wants to talk with an executive assistant—sounds more like a boyfriend than a vendor. Mary has become an expert at picturing the people she speaks with, them sitting at their desks, holding their phones. Sometimes she feels she can see through their voices, into their marriages, their weekends. She knows they can't see through her.

With a slow scan of her desk, she wonders. Where are all the other pictures? Her other kids? She'd wanted a houseful of kids, but when Ted lost his job they needed money, and he'd told her that on her salary they couldn't afford more rug rats. He was right, and she couldn't have stayed home to raise them anyway. But she still wanted more pictures, like on the other desks.

Nothing worse than a slow day.

In twelve years she'll be allowed to retire. She'll probably still put on her face each morning, even though there will be no more need to sound or look cheery. Maybe she'll start drinking with Ted. Maybe they'll get along better then; they'll have something in common. By then Charlotte's baby will be a kid. Maybe there'll be more kids. Maybe a houseful.

At home she owns a Conair Slimline with pushbuttons on the handle. She bought it when the model first came out, to replace the old rotary. But that Conair hates her with each button's shrill beep, so she doesn't make calls.

Ted had told her that when she retires, she better get a hobby. She told him he's got his. He shouted at her to screw off and hit her. Luckily he was off balance and missed mostly; nothing foundation can't fix.

She likes thinking about learning to knit; it looks peaceful, her fingers moving, like pushing buttons. Pianos. As a girl she'd taken lessons, liked imagining herself in a concert hall, but the lessons got hard and fell away.

Mary tugs down on her blouse, giving it a good straightening, firming it against her breasts; someone might come in to talk with her.

Jim Sunderland, from Accounts Payable in the Spares Department, used to hang around the lobby. He'd ask about her day, and lean over the counter farther than he needed while looking down at her. Mary would lean forward farther than she needed. She felt dirty and excited. She would keep looking down at the phone so Jim couldn't see her face flush. Jim retired years ago.

"What are you looking at?" she snaps at Ted's picture. Other than occasional banging from the remodel, the walls resonate with silence.

Lunch hangs an hour away. She sits up and straightens her blouse again; nothing blinks.

Addiction

I remember being worth more alive than dead,
according to my financial planner.
Now only my minister tells me so.
Her voice filters through the sweltering choir
squatting in my head.
Self-loathing lullabies of hot hopeless futures
blare within my skull's thin walls.

Gurgling shadows flow toward a crevice,
where the steaming cleavage seduces
with its ample oblivion.

No horizon to latch on to.
A whirlpool drives my unhinged thirst.
Powerless,
I spin.

Note: By the grace of God, and the twelve steps of AA, as of this writing the
poet hasn't taken a drink in over fifteen years.

Journey in a Dream

With frayed strands of rope
digging into my shoulder
I drag a rotted rowboat
through tall desert dunes.

A bleached hull with splintered
planks grates across the sand,
each rough timber
a testament to friction.

Passing squatting beggars,
I overhear one say,
"He's so stupid,
he'll probably forget to die."

Where Poems Live

Poems fill voids,
cavities between thoughts.
Their relentless substance
grasps for cool air.

As mortar gives purpose to brick,
words construct our architecture.
Ancient generations laid the
masonry of our parapets.

We tell time by a crack or crevasse.
Those eroded by life
create the space
for more poems.

Big Money[F]

You take aim and toss the iron grappling hook toward a bright orange buoy floating near the boat. The grapple snags the line and you pull in the buoy. This is your first pull of the king crab season on the Bering Sea. The water is dusky blue, and over the waves white froth blows glistening in the sun: that cold polished wind, the air you love. Inhaling the sky with every breath.

After pushing the black lever that sets the puller wheels spinning, the line attached to the buoy shoots onboard like a mad snake. The other end is attached to a metal crab pot two hundred feet down.

Behind you, hunched over and covered hood-to-toe in yellow raingear, Eddie grabs that line and slaps down sections so they fall onto the deck in a coil. When the pot eventually breaks the surface, Fritz slings a hook from the picking boom into the bridle and hoists the pot so it hangs over the deck, as you grab the pot's rebar frame. The phone-booth sized trap falls to the deck. Fritz opens the pot doors and starts pulling out purple crab that look like giant spiders.

The pot is packed so tightly with crab that the spines on their legs are locking them together. You reach in wearing blue rubber gloves and start grabbing the spindles of alien legs flaying at the air. There's an aluminum hopper nearby where you drop the crab one at a time into the live tank, where they sink and disappear. You always want to toss them in, it's faster and there are more than a hundred crabs, but the skipper will start yelling from the pilothouse how much each crab is worth and that they've got to be alive or the cannery won't buy them. And he's right; these are worth a ton. In just five minutes of working, your share of this pot is a hundred bucks.

And there are fifty more pots in this string, plus another string already on the bottom just waiting to be picked, and—holy shit—there are eight weeks left in the season. The day is swinging and you can see making a hundred grand in a hurry. Just knowing that pumps up your heart and makes you horny.

Pitching isn't really the word for what the boat is doing. It's more like a punch-drunk fighter being pummeled by the waves. You've always got a wide stance so you don't topple over. That's ok. It's kind of fun to rock and roll with the sea, especially knowing the cash is flowing in.

The last crab is out and Fritz is half-crawling into the pot to attach new bait. Fritz is out. The pot door is closed. You push the lever that tips the pot launcher so the rusty cage slides back into the water. That was easy.

Now it's time to move fast. The rest of the line is still on deck and you've got to gather it up and throw it over—before the seven-hundred-pound pot starts pulling rope straight off the deck.

With gusts whistling through the rigging, engines thumping, waves roiling onto themselves, and you throwing line over the side as fast as you can, there's hardly room to wedge in a thought.

"What the hell!" Eddie shouts, and you look up to see he's being showered with hydraulic oil from a burst fitting high on the picking boom. He starts sliding, slipping across the oiled deck. For an instant you think he looks like a circus clown, flapping his arms and falling on his big yellow butt.

Not good. That oil will spread in a heartbeat and no one will be standing. You're closest to the controls and take a quick step to shut off the rain of oil.

That's when you feel it—the bite.

Your ankle sparks as the line wraps around your boot and instantly tightens with the full weight of the sinking pot. Once your feet are yanked out, the back of your head smacks the deck causing a blast of light within your skull. For a second, you're able to keep a desperate grasp of the railing.

During your time in the air, before hitting the water, knowing how cold it will be, how unavoidable…you take a desperate gasp, and suck in salty spray.

Bubbles. All sound is bubbles. It's not cold, not like jumping into a lake. Your raingear presses against you offering insulation, until a pant leg billows open and the water rushes in, cold as an ice pick spiking up your calf and inner thighs, assaulting your torso and shocking your armpits to clamp down.

They saw you go in. You know they'll grab the line, haul you up—unless all the line's been pulled over while they slid around the oily deck. You're desperate to feel that bite tighten to bone breaking when they start pulling from their end.

The sting of brine fills deep into your sinuses.

You remember calling home. You always, no matter what, ended those calls with "I love you."

Your chest feels as if it's going to explode as your stomach rocks and twists in knots. Overpowering any fear, you strain forward, trying to grab your boot and pull it off. With a pure burst of power to reach down…you get nothing, other than expelling your last bit of breath.

All you can do is scream. Your mouth stretches wide open over and over but can't make noise. Weak as shadows, your arms flail as you plummet into the dark.

A thought hemorrhages: "Is this it?" Even if they start pulling from the surface, you're not sure you'd last long enough to get there.

Inhale! Inhale? Yes!

An incurable pull expands your chest, flooding you with relief, followed by lightning ricocheting throughout your lungs: snapping, burning pain. Then limp. No fighting. There's quiet.

Your mind searches the forsaken blackness—floating weightless in an opaque void. Where's the light? The welcoming light? There's supposed to be a light.

Note: Yes, I applied at Home Depot. They called me in, but didn't hire me. I wrote the letter below just after finishing my real cover letter. The people who work at Home Depot are fine, doing honest work and supporting their families. Apparently, I had some self-image issues.

Dear Home Depot HR:

I'm one of those old people who is burned out and no longer much good to society, so I'd like to work at Home Depot. I can envision myself helping a customer, but just before they speak, I look at my walkie-talkie and frown—then walk away.

On those frequent occasions when I can't remember where something is, with supreme confidence I'll tell the customer it's in the farthest corner from wherever I'm standing. Should I see them in the store again, I'll tell them that was my stupid twin brother and direct them to another remote corner.

I know I won't be at the top of the corporate ladder. But I'm perfectly satisfied if I have only a single person to supervise, someone who can do most of my work, take all of the blame, and find me when I get lost.

Concerning that person I supervise: they can't be too short. Short people creep me out; they're like dolls with wet eyes. (My psychiatrist says I'll never get over this.)

I don't believe it's not shoplifting if you don't get caught, but I do understand there are certain employee perks when my home needs so many repairs, just like yours, I'm sure.

I like watching birds when they get caught in a store and fly around the rafters. They can keep me entertained for hours.

All yours,
Steve Theme

Cemetery Song

She stands as wisps of clouds blow
where her thick black hair once flourished.
He loved running his fingers through that soft forest.
Now, fresh-turned dirt tints the wind, and spring's green vigor
surrounds three generations.
A boy with peach fuzz lifts his face
from his mother's wet shoulder.
"He was the best grandpa in the whole world."
Mom echoes "And the moon."
A light chuckle ripples the black fabrics.

Large in his suit, a salt and pepper gentleman reaches for his
    sister's hand,
one he hasn't held since walking to grade school.
They look to each other, both with their father's eyes.

Reaching into the red purse he'd given her for their fiftieth,
hands gnarled from holding his, she pulls out leaflets, and passes
    them left and right.
As the papers circulate, she remains iron straight and gazes into
    the eternal blue.
Her eyes rest back on family with a fresh smile.
"Let's sing."

I'll fly away, oh glory
I'll fly away, in the morning
When I die
Hallelujah, bye and bye
I'll fly away

Tears cascade over smiling cheeks.

Out to Lunch

The window sucks my sight through it
scattering sky blues over the horizon.
They slink in a daydream to the
shadowed hemisphere, where daydreams
are just dreams. My view lolls,
lost in the shadow.

An astral breeze swings my scattered
vision over an obsidian sea the
the sun can't touch. Mountains like rumpled
linen glide beneath me, while vast
plains lead to a distant skyline.

Daylight leans on the shadow
as throngs of clouds reach
red with tentacles, wet and
raining to the rich earth, as I come
white-hot through the atmosphere
to settle here,
at this black desk,
on time and smiling.

The Parable of the Mother and Son

One summer afternoon a mother and her little boy were walking on the beach. She had just bought him an ice cream cone. The large ball of ice cream balanced atop the cone and when he excitedly reached for his first bite, he knocked off the ice cream. Looking down at it covered in sand and ruined, he launched into hysterics, crying unconsolably. His mother understood why he was crying, and knew he should be crying. She comforted him, but also understood that although this seems tragic to him now, as he grows and gains new perspectives this isn't as tragic an event as the boy may think. In time he too would understand. Telling the boy that someday he'd understand would be of no help in the moment, so she keeps that to herself.

They eventually left the beach and when crossing a road, a drunk driver hit the little boy and killed him. Looking down at this body, the mother launched into hysterics, crying unconsolably. All of the angels of heaven understood why she was crying, and knew she should be crying. If sought, they were available to console her, but they understood although this seems tragic to her now, as she grows to someday join them and gain new perspectives, this isn't as tragic an event as the mother may think. In time she too would understand. Telling her that someday she'd understand would be of no help in the moment, so they keep that to themselves.

* * *

We think of ourselves as adults but in fact are not yet even born. We are gestating. That which awaits exists beyond this universe where our authentic selves—stripped of gender, money, ethnicity, age, want and all other earthly markers—can live within the ocean of love and acceptance that springs from a timeless eternity.

Proof

Children are proof
God wants us to love each other.
Death is proof
God loves us.

The Silent Violin^F

Sweat. This stadium smells like acrid anxiety, with all these people standing in line. Everyone short of breath. Feels like there is an unbalanced motor revving in my chest; more crying and wailing here than I expected. There must be fifty thousand of us, a drop in the bucket. Maybe a village or two hidden in Borneo won't stand in some line, but that's about it. There are probably twenty-five lines at this arena. This is the first time I wish a line would slow down.

So many people, yet the stands are empty. This is no sports crowd. A lot of crosses, others with yarmulkes, some with rosaries, and one guy burning incense he snuck past security. I've brough a picture of my wife and kids. No electronics allowed. We're cut off from those not here. Families don't come except to escort young children. No spouses or friends, just random selection. The woman in front of me is elderly, small; she doesn't turn to look at me.

No one thought it would come to this. It's not as if we did anything wrong. We're just humans. Definitely a case of too much of a good thing. With every breath it's like I'm breathing someone else's air.

Everyone reports. Everywhere. Every town, every state, every man, woman and child—every nation. That will cover all 14 billion of us. In only four more years there'll be 16. Each billion comes faster than the one before it. We tried seeding the oceans, built oxygen generation stations. Studies show it may already be too late. It's been at least fifteen years that most healthy people have been impacted by ODS, oxygen deficiency syndrome—every human on the globe. This isn't like global warming; there are no deniers this time. Every gasping breath reinforces the reality.

The previous generations thought if we reduced CO_2 levels, everything would go back to normal. We believed that because we desperately wanted to.

Life's not that simple.

We were able to leave fossil fuels behind, but the oceans had already begun to acidify. Even though we were able to cut way back, with all the CO_2 already in the atmosphere it just continued dissolving into the oceans, creating carbonic acid. Ocean plankton have always generated the huge bulk of the oxygen for the entire planet and finally the acid killed enough of them that O_2 levels started dropping. How were we going to stop that? Cover the oceans?

It took years to get really bad, but everything's connected. Combine that with our millions of livestock, the acreage we dominate, the resources we use, and especially the forests we leveled—humans have managed to kill the living partners we rely on for survival. Everything in the oceans has been harmed, but now even some bird species are starting to die. Coming to grips has been hell for everyone. No one ever thought we'd run out of oxygen.

* * *

There was talk of using electrolysis to create oxygen from water. There's no way we can generate enough to spread across the entire globe—up through the clouds, across the oceans and sustain all the animals. That doesn't really matter though since most of the manufactured O_2 is being horded by the super-rich.

Scientists say half of us must go so the other half can survive, or at least have a better chance. So today is the day, at least for me. Everyone is told to get their affairs in order, say their goodbyes. Only half of us here will go home today.

For my kids, their entire lives have been spent without enough oxygen. At least not as much as I or my parents enjoyed growing up. We used to visit parks and walk through the woods. Not anymore, not for years. It's a constant grind and I always feel guilty when I see them sitting around for hours. They're just kids! They want to run around and play, but they don't. None do.

There's a plan for the orphans, but I hope Jackhi and Bellame aren't part of it. Chelwan has another week and the kids will go in with her. We've talked, a lot, trying to reach some kind of peace, but I'm not there. Theoretically two of us will make it, but it could be all four, maybe none. I hope it's not only one.

At home, the four of us have taken to sitting in a circle and we each tell a story. The stories can be long, short, serious, loud, ridiculous, full of voices, waving arms, you name it. Bellame is telling an epic adventure she builds on each day. I'm one of the kings in her land. Jackhi has started telling us of the adventures of two buddies. Their names are Stinky and Slimy. Yesterday they met Queen Elizabeth while in a hot air balloon. I don't know where he gets the fortitude to still make us laugh, at least until we start gasping.

* * *

Just depends on the flip of a coin. I can't believe we're using coins, but we don't have time to build an ornate global selection system. Of course some people are trying to cheat and hide; others are volunteering.

I can see the yellow line. That's where we wait while the person ahead flips the coin. Before the coin they step behind a curtain into what looks like an oversized voting booth. The closer I get to the yellow line, the quieter everyone is becoming.

No one talks now, not a word here, just labored beathing. More and more you can see people who have suffered permanent mental impairment. I was thinking people would be freaking out, but no one has any energy. We look like cattle walking to slaughter: heads down, some moaning, crowded, and unsure where we're going.

Like everywhere else, we wait at the yellow line. When it's our turn, we step up. But here it's not like stepping up to a DMV window. We're stepping up to the clamp.

One wrist goes into the clamp; the other hand flips the coin. If it's heads you walk—if it's tails, the Volunteer sprays the clamped hand with blue ink. That's the marker in case you figure a way to run, but there's no running, you're already clamped. All of the Volunteers have blue hands. They make sure everyone will do their part. If I'm inked, I'll be put into a holding room and they'll take me to a processing center tonight.

So much seems pointless, all the hard work. Hard work. That's what my father said. "With hard work you can make something of yourself."

I made myself an obstetrician. Wanted to help people, and wanted to make money. Over the years I'm not totally sure which one of those was the primary reason. I like to think it's fifty/fifty, but even that might be a stretch. Of course being a doc is rewarding, but now it seems that fear drove many of my choices. Thinking of myself as old and poor terrified me. Now, all that fear may have been for nothing, like most of my fears.

When we met, Chelwan worked as a nurse in the Labor and Delivery Unit. We used to joke that with all the babies she had a guaranteed job for life, but when Jackhi was born she quit. Taking care of the kids absorbed her every fiber. I've seen so many moms, and in my professional opinion, she's the pinnacle. When Bellame contracted the meningitis that damaged her hearing, the kids couldn't figure how Chelwan would let that happen. Now they're old enough to know the disease wasn't their mom's fault. They know this isn't their mom's fault, either.

My black loafers stand out against the yellow. They remind me of two flies stuck in honey. Nothing is in my control.

Control. Soon I won't control even what my hands are doing. Haven't been able to control my breathing for years—it's never right. What's going to happen to my family? I want to beg for mercy. I'll beg just to be allowed to beg, but beseech whom? No one is exempt.

I can hear the notes, so clear and sustained. It's like the bow is in my hand. I remember as a boy thinking I'd play my violin in a symphony. In high school I spent more time with my violin than with my friends. That was really my first love, not medicine. Getting lost in the music came so easily. Played consistently for thirteen years but the thought of trying to make any money, to actually survive as a violinist—I ran from it. Medical school seemed the safer and more acceptable route. Now my violin just sits as a prop on a bookshelf, but sometimes I look at it and daydream. When I played, what I really loved…

It's time.

The clamp is warm and wet from all the wrists. I get one flip.

Miracles & Mysteries

I delivered this sermon at the Cedar Hills United Church of Christ, in Portland, Oregon, on August 15, 2021. I'm not ordained in any religion.

I'd like to thank Mary Sue, JJ, and the Worship Committee for giving me this opportunity once again to speak from the pulpit. I'm going to tell a story and then give the sermon. In other churches this story could be called testifying, but we don't really do that in the UCC. However, what you're about to hear is a testament to the power of prayer and God's compassion.

In the past I've mentioned this story to a number of people in our church; however, no one knows the full story. Today, you all will know all of it.

This begins in Mexico, in August, with heat in the upper 90's. In 2008 our youth group had driven down south of Tijuana to build a home for a family that really needed one. All our work was completed by hand. We dug the foundation; mixed the concrete; cut eight foot lengths of plywood; cut the framing, siding, roofing—everything done by hand, no power tools. We had five days to build an entire home from digging the foundation to tar-papering the roof.

The location was dusty and exposed, not a single tree for shade. The family lived in a shack next to the job site. The parents had three children. They could afford for only one daughter to attend school. The other two kids were illiterate, as were the parents.

Again, this was Mexico, in August. At night we slept in tents in a dirt parking lot. Here too, there was nothing for shade, just a large barren lot with some latrines and an outdoor shower, if you brought your own bag of water.

During the days we worked hard in the direct sun. At lunch our group piled into the back of our family minivan, which had all the seats removed. It was basically a hot metal box but it was also the only place with any shade. By the end of the first day we all felt great, had worked hard, and made good progress.

By the end of the second day, I noticed some extra fatigue, but that was to be expected since we were working hard and sleep wasn't that great in a stuffy warm tent. By the third day I was pretty much soaked in sweat before lunch. At one point I felt compelled to stand in a barrel of water to try and cool off, which I later found out was the family's drinking water. (Yes, we refreshed it.)

By the end of the fourth day I was in bad shape. I drove from the job site, but I shouldn't have. I couldn't think, at times felt numb, was weak, confused, was nauseous and had no appetite for dinner. When we got back to camp, I was thankful I hadn't crashed the van driving back and went to my hot tent where I remained until breakfast.

According to the website of the Mayo Clinic, "Having heat exhaustion one day can predispose an individual to heat illness the next day." It suggests getting out of the sun, remaining in an air-conditioned building, or maybe enjoying a cool bath…not happening where we were.

The website also notes that the older you are, the more susceptible you are to heat exhaustion or heat stroke. Now I was the oldest member of our group, but apparently not old enough to have the wisdom to recognize my deteriorating condition. Several websites state, in bold, that heat exhaustion can lead to heat stroke, which is an emergency that requires immediate medical help, or death may ensue.

We were now on our fifth and last dusty day. I worked until lunch and after the kids cleared out of the back of the van I crawled in and laid down. The van might have been a little bit cooler than hell, but hard to say. The back hatch was swung open and I was lying on my back staring at the ceiling. After a while my oldest son, Mattson, came up and asked how I was doing. My response was going to be that I was ok, just needed a bit more time in the shade and I'd be back out working. I wanted to tip my head up to look at him as I said this, and not just stare at the ceiling with no eye contact, but when I tried to look at him, I didn't have the strength to lift my head. I tried harder but still no movement. So I gave him my weak words of assurance that I'd be out soon.

As he left my heart sank. I now knew I was done for the entire day. I was useless and we still had a lot to complete. The windows weren't in, the front door needed to be hung, the roof wasn't done and the whole house still needed stucco applied to the sides. If we didn't finish there were no other groups coming behind us to complete the job. As it stood, the house wasn't yet ready to protect them from wind or rain.

The Bible doesn't lack for miracles, and the book of Acts is jammed full of them. I call one of my favorites, "the miracle for parents of teenagers." This appears in Acts 9 when Peter is in Lydda and comes across a man named Aeneas who had been bed-ridden for eight years. Peter says to him, "Aeneas, Jesus Christ heals you! Get up and make your bed." Aeneas then rises to his feet at once and makes his bed. I can see myself saying that to one of my boys as a teenager. The miracle wouldn't be if he rose up, *but if he made his bed!* He did it! It's a miracle. Praise the Lord!

These types of miracles are obvious and clear. Many miracles aren't as obvious, but equally miraculous. Like the miracle of birth. The miracle of life itself. There's not one biologist or botanist who can say what makes a blade of grass grow. They can describe the chemical reactions once it starts growing, but none can explain the life force that initiates the whole process.

Given that the definition of a miracle is something that we can't explain, I'd offer that every blade of grass is a miracle. A spawning salmon will use its ultimate last bit of energy working to ensure the next generation survives. That's a miracle. All of us are miracles: our children are miracles, as are our friends and family.

We're surrounded by so many miracles we can't see the forest for the trees. Trees are miracles. We have miracles blocking our view of miracles!

So there I am, lying in back of this sweltering van, staring at the ceiling unable to move. In retrospect, I was clearly in the middle of a medical emergency. We probably weren't going to finish the home, and I was absolutely useless. Each morning the family welcomed us as their excitement and gratitude kept growing. Now we were going to let them down. In my despair, I said a prayer. This is it, verbatim: "God, there is so much left to do, and so little time, how can I help?"

As with the story of Aeneas, the answer was unambiguous and immediate. And by immediate I don't mean within one minute, or even a few seconds. I mean immediate! (I snapped my fingers.) I felt all my strength return; the dizziness vanished, the nausea vanished, and the confusion vanished. Remember, this was day four of heat exhaustion.

So I thought I'd try to prop up on my elbow, certain that once my head lifted a bit that I'd pass out, but I'd try anyway, since I wouldn't have far to fall. Once propped on my elbow and still remaining conscious, I thought I'd sit up, and figured it was guaranteed I'd blackout then. But again, the fall wouldn't be that far, so I tried. To my surprise I found myself sitting upright and still conscious. So I thought, what the heck, I may as well try standing and maybe I won't pass out. So I stood, and there I was feeling perfectly fine. I strode down to the house and spent the rest of the afternoon, in the direct sun, on a ladder, applying stucco to the walls. Before we left, the family had a completed home. That night I proceeded to eat a full dinner and felt fine for the rest of the trip.

That was 14 years ago and just last year I was looking at some pictures from that mission trip. There's one shot taken at the end of the last day just before I got in the van to drive away. On my chest there is an image made from wet sweat, a salt ring from dried sweat, and dust. I hadn't noticed this before, but it doesn't take any imagination to see the angel there, flying up and to the left into the clouds. See the wings spread across my chest?

Is this what angels look like? I don't know, but they know we think they look like that. I believe heaven will always speak to us in a language we understand.

I've walked this earth for sixty-three years, and on any other day, even just one day before or after, I'd see this image on my chest as an interesting coincidence. But my brothers and sisters, not on this day. This is no coincidence. This is an angel's calling card.

So here I am, with a smile on my face and an angel on my chest, when in all likelihood I probably should have been dead. That's the end of the story.

* * *

Now for the sermon. Don't worry, it's short. In fact, it's only one sentence. But since this is the sermon, I'm going to lay my foot heavy on the preacher pedal. This isn't a suggestion, or a recommendation. As my father used to say, I'm not asking you to do this:

Live a life worthy of the miracles you have received.
Once more, so you can remember the entire sermon.
Live a life worthy of the miracles you have received.

Amen.

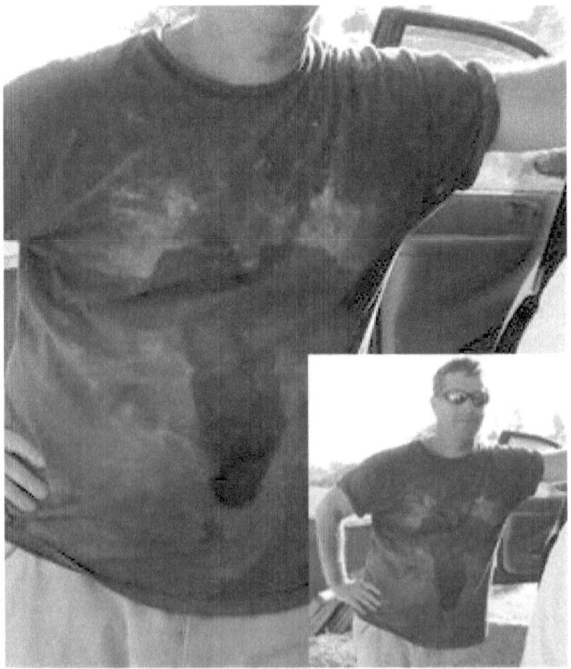

Photo by Robin Jackson.

Acknowledgments

The author would like to thank the following for contributing their time and talent to this book: Ann Farley, Bruce Gulliver, Coyote Club, Darren Howard, Elana Thieme, Frank Hicks, Jim Woodruff, J.S. James, John Fugett, Kenneth Cale, Katie Bennett, Lou Maenz, Mary Williams, Mattson Thieme, Michele Koh Morollo, Ronda Struth, Ross West, Susan Parman, Tom Klonoski, Vinnie Kinsella, and Willamette Writers.

About Halyard Press

A halyard is the rope used to raise a sail. We hope our work raises spirits and helps readers continue on their spiritual journeys. We have no motto or catchy tag line, but we have a guiding principle—be of service.

HalyardPress.com